Matthew Markell is a licensed master's level therapist in the State of Washington, residing in the Seattle area. Combining his love of human healing, growth, storytelling, human psychology, and mythology, Matthew integrates storytelling and personal narrative healing into his therapeutic practice. In addition to his private practice, he also conducts day-long journaling-workshop intensives, teaching people how to use the skills of storytelling and personal narratives to contribute toward continued healing and personal growth.

This book is dedicated to the memory of David P. Markell

Matthew Markell

THE FIRE THAT NEVER DIES

Dragons of the West

AUSTIN MACAULEY PUBLISHERS™

LONDON ∗ CAMBRIDGE ∗ NEW YORK ∗ SHARJAH

Ordering Information
Quantity sales: Special discounts are available on quantity purchases by corporations, associations, and others. For details, contact the publisher at the address below.

Publisher's Cataloguing-in-Publication data
Markell, Matthew
The Fire That Never Dies

ISBN 9781647501556 (Paperback)
ISBN 9781647501549 (Hardback)
ISBN 9781647501563 (ePub e-book)

Library of Congress Control Number: 2020925352

www.austinmacauley.com/us

First Published (2021)
Austin Macauley Publishers LLC
40 Wall Street, 33rd Floor, Suite 3302
New York, NY 10005
USA

mail-usa@austinmacauley.com
+1 (646) 5125767

I would like to thank Dr. Harley Ferris and Dr. Kamala Randolph for reviewing the manuscript and offering analysis, critique, insight, and support. I would also like to thank the many mentors in my life who have taught me something important about the art of dragon-taming—Rick, Steve, Doug, and Bear. I would like to thank Ramon Deslauriers for his stunning original artwork for the book cover. Finally, I would like to thank my family for their encouragement and support throughout the writing process.

Table of Contents

Introduction

The great myths and legends that have been passed down to us through countless generations are more than just interesting stories or morality plays. Rather, they are timeless tales that reveal to us the deepest and most enduring truths of the human condition. The myth is that which mirrors back to us our true nature; the fullness of who and what we are. The various characters and creatures of myth symbolize different parts of the human experience and psyche. Some of these characters and creatures inspire deep love, awe, and devotion in us, while others inspire terror, suspicion, and disgust. Myths do not allow us to simply see the parts of ourselves we like and want to see. They also reveal to us the darker aspects of our nature, those aspects that, at first glance, we are tempted to regard as threatening, evil or ugly. Myths force us to contend with these aspects of ourselves.

These fascinating tales carry our own projections of the human experience and feed them back to us in a way that our waking consciousness can make sense of and begin to grapple with. They offer us a window into the vast and untamed wilderness of our own souls, both to let us know what resides there and also to give us clues about how we should learn to greet all of the different parts of ourselves as we find them mirrored in the characters, creatures and settings of these timeless tales. Our great myths are timeless, because they are the stories of "us."

Great tales of heroism, love, self-sacrifice, bravery and a longing to discover and explore some distant land, inform us that we have a purpose to our existence that includes a quest of some kind. These quests lure us away from home; that place which is safe and familiar to us. Myths tell us that we have some business to attend to in the wilderness. The wilderness is the unknown and untamed place. It is a place we retreat to for refuge as well as a place we seek refuge from. It can be a place of both rest and enlightenment as well as that of danger and even death. The wilderness does not conform to our expectations of what we should like it to be. It tells the naked truth. It has no hidden agenda, and yet it holds great mysteries and timeless stories that stretch back into time, well before any human language or symbol was around to bear witness to it. We find ourselves drawn to it for this and many other reasons.

The wilderness is also home to all of the wild creatures that inhabit both the earth and the worlds of myth. I believe we instinctually reach toward these places, and the creatures that inhabit them, when we are feeling "stuck" somewhere in our lives and it becomes time for us to move along from that which has become safe, comfortable and familiar to us. The wilderness holds the stories about us that we are not telling. Some of these stories are emerging from within us for the first time, while some are ancient and long-forgotten. Some are stories that have laid dormant, waiting for the proper moment to reveal themselves, and some are long overdue stories, waiting to break into our consciousness, but have found a strong resistance within us because we are frightened of how we might have to change once those stories reveal themselves to us.

The world of myth is a wilderness of its own. Most of the truths of who we are remain hidden to us for various reasons. Some of what is hidden from us is that which we have not yet been ready to see. Much of it is that which we choose not to see. Carl Jung's term for this place within the human psyche is called the "Shadow," and the shadow, or the unconscious parts of ourselves, are primordial regions of the wild. We are both fascinated with and terrified of these places all at the same time.

Dragons are archetypal creatures of this hidden wilderness. While dragons in the great myths and legends are all very diverse in their appearance and purpose, they are nonetheless to be found in one form or another in almost every great mythology around the world. This, of course, is what makes them such an instantly recognizable symbol. They are universal, even as they are incredibly complex and diverse in appearance and purpose. Depending on where one is in the world, a dragon can represent great evil or great wisdom. In all traditions, dragons are untamed and capable of causing trouble, whether that trouble is designed to help us or destroy us.

Why dragons? It is precisely because these creatures of the wild appear so threatening and so powerful to us that they get our attention quickly. One's natural instinct when faced with a creature of such immense power and fright is to fight it or flee from it. This fight or flight instinct is an evolutionary one that we have developed as a species to promote our survival, allowing us to live and thrive in a wild and untamed world. In the outer world, it is a helpful instinct for us to have. When it comes to the inner world, however, this fight or flight instinct works against us.

When one moves into the realm of the inner world, one also moves into the strange world of myth and the symbols they produce. This world does not operate under the same rules of nature and logic that we have learned to successfully apprehend in our daily lives, which is part of the reason why our fight or flight instincts do not work for us there. All of the characters and creatures of fairy tale and legend have wisdom and knowledge to share with us about the nature of the diverse elements of the individual Psyche. It is important that we get to know all of the different parts of ourselves as intimately as we possibly can, including those that we do not like or are frightened of. Myths provide us with a means to learn how to do this.

We have some idea of how these inner characters work and express themselves. Some examples of personification, that many of us are familiar with today, might include an "inner critic," a "frightened child," or a "perfectionist," as well as a "brave soul," a "generous heart," or a "strong warrior." These motifs, and many more, are embodied in the symbols of the different characters and creatures residing in all our myths and legends. The fantastical nature and drama of these characters and creatures serves the purpose of grabbing our attention.

Dragons, being already powerful in our imaginations, arrive to us as creatures from that great wilderness of our unconscious selves (as do all manner of Shadow creatures) as emissaries.

Dragons have a tendency to appear when the shadow parts of our personality have already tried subtler ways of getting our attention and failed. Now is when the Unconscious gets serious and begins to send something more frightening like a dragon our way that will do a better job of getting our attention, making it more difficult for us to ignore it.

The problem with fighting or fleeing these inner dragons is that both of these responses only make them grow more powerful and dangerous in an attempt to wake us up and pay attention. This leaves us with the necessity to develop a different response when dealing with our dragons. We must, instead, face the dragon; not to conquer or slay it, but to befriend it. This may feel like a "taming" of the dragon, and in a sense, this is true, as we work to shift its allegiance from being our antagonist to our ally. What we are not doing, however, is domesticating our dragons, as it is their wild and untamed natures that we must make more room for in our inner lives. Our dragons will not allow us to try to domesticate them in any case. They require our deepest respect and loyalty. Only then will they consent to switching their allegiance from our antagonist to our ally. Our dragons, as long as we continue to honor, respect, and treat them wisely, can provide us with an endless source of wisdom and strength.

In this book, the question we are asking is how do people of Western cultures with an inheritance of Western myths go about the process of taming and befriending dragons? While Eastern myths and legends about dragons are already very familiar with the idea of dragon-taming, no dragons that emerge in any of our Western myths are perceived as wise or potentially helpful to human beings. They are always, and only, creatures of wrath and chaos, and must be fought and slain, or failing this, fled from. Taming dragons is not an idea or a virtue that has yet occurred to us in the Western, mythic imagination.

While I do believe it is to our benefit to familiarize ourselves with Eastern myths and dragons, I do not believe we can merely mimic or appropriate their methods, as there are fundamentally different assumptions about human nature and the human psyche that have arisen between Eastern and Western cultures. Neither one is good or bad or better than the other. It is simply the recognition that they are different. To ignore our own history and mythology as Western people would be a form of evading our own Shadows, which would defeat the purpose of getting to know our own dragons. We must, in some ways, develop our own understanding and hence, our own methods of dragon-taming in order for the process to work properly. It is to this end that I write this book, which sets about the task of learning how to ask the right questions to teach us how to tame and befriend our own dragons.

In this book, we will learn to employ the value and ethics of curiosity, acceptance and compassion of all of our inner parts, working under the assumption that they all belong to us and that they all have something important to teach us about ourselves that is necessary for our own growth and well-being. This includes our dragons and other such creatures of shadow that our vast, unconscious psyches produce; reflected back to us through our myths and other means of external projections.

The creatures of our shadows are a part of us and belong to us. As such, we cannot ignore them nor can we simply get rid of them. The longer we try to employ either approach, the more voracious and irascible our dragons will become, until they finally succeed in getting our attention. Our dragons are a part of us. When we choose to fight them, we are fighting ourselves. Our own dragons may feel threatening, dangerous and unruly to us, but they have something to offer that we need in order to keep growing and learning in both wisdom and abundance. They are of great importance to us and learning how to value and nurture them appropriately is one of our tasks in life.

Our dragons are agents of transformation and change. They bring to our attention the right tasks, or better yet—the right conundrums—we must face at just the right times in life. These are not events that we can anticipate or choreograph. These impulses are functions of the Ego, which we will explore later in the book. The nature of the transformation that occurs in these moments also cannot be anticipated, because when we do this, we are bringing our own assumptions about change and transformation to bear on the outcome, when it is some of our fundamental assumptions about ourselves and the nature of change that must be transformed in the first place.

As we grow up, we all learn how to become fragmented, cutting off parts of ourselves that don't belong to the ideal versions of ourselves, we are working hard to create and promote. As such, we begin to experience an inner sense of brokenness and woundedness. The presence of dragons in our lives ensures that we never give up on the ongoing inner reconciliation process we are all tasked to undergo, as we come to terms with all the different and diverse parts of our own personalities, particularly the ones we have rejected. Our dragons teach us, however unhappy we may be about it at times, that we cannot ignore or omit the parts of ourselves we do not like or are afraid of, as we all do our own work toward inner healing and reconciliation.

Our dragons are designed to wake us up and push us out of the nests of our innocence, comfort and allegiance to the status quo. They teach us both the reality and value of death as a necessary part of life. For, without an ability to die and learn to live again, we cannot grow. Our dragons are not content to let us get away with anything less than the fullest expression of who and what we already are, and who we are becoming. That is the gift they bring to us. Our dragons come to gather us up when we have been neglecting the wild places in our own souls for too long. How we learn to greet and work with our own dragons, will make all the difference in whether we choose to accept the journeys of our own growth and inner reconciliation, or whether we remain stuck and fragmented throughout the remainder of our lives.

Dragon work is soul work. For the purposes of this book, I will use the terms "Soul," "Self," and "Psyche" interchangeably with each other, as all of them describe the fullness of the human experience and represent the original wholeness from which we all come. As we grow up and learn how to manage the world (both the outer world and the inner world), we become fragmented and isolated from ourselves, and we see this same experience replicated in our relationships with other people as well. While this is not a pleasant experience, there is a reason for why we must first go through a process of inner fragmentation. We begin our lives in a state of both wholeness and innocence, and there is something we are meant to learn about taking that journey into experience and the dangers of the inner fragmentation it poses, that gives us the necessary gifts to return to that state of wholeness with conscious awareness.

This is the work of the "Hero's Journey," eloquently and exhaustively described by the great Joseph Campbell. The great stories and myths are the vehicles we use to guide us through the treacherous landscape of experience

15

and fragmentation, only to bring us right back to where we started. The scenery may look the same, but we have changed, and our transformation has not taken us further away from ourselves but brought us back to them with full consciousness and awareness. It is not through neglecting our wounds that we heal them. It is through learning how to engage with them in full conscious awareness, and allowing them to transform us into deeper vessels for love, compassion, courage, and wisdom.

Myths are projections. They capture the unconscious stories about ourselves that we have lost or abandoned and feed them back to us in the form of a drama that captures our attention and stirs our imagination. Myths employ many symbols to invoke our emotions, as well as many interesting characters and creatures. The meaning of these symbols may not be immediately apparent to us, but as we learn how to live with them and interact with them consciously, we can begin to understand the wisdom they intend to convey to us with time.

In this book, we will explore the symbols, meaning and purpose of dragons. While dragons may be instantly recognizable to us as threats, to be feared or hated, this book will encourage us to cultivate a new sense of courage which allows us to question these assumptions and invites us to develop a different response to our dragons. This book is dedicated to exploring some of the fiery symbols that awaken to us the knowledge of our own dragons and the potential gifts they have to offer us as individuals, and what this knowledge has to offer to the wider world around us as well.

In order for us to explore our dragons properly, we must have a good foundation upon which to understand our current relationship with dragons. The first part of the book is dedicated to exploring our past, taking a look at some of our Western myths and how they have informed the Western (or Occidental) Psyche over time. Without any knowledge of our inheritance, we begin this quest with one hand tied behind our backs, as it were. We need to understand the stories of where we come from and how those stories were created. The second part of the book takes a closer look at specific dragon myths from different parts of our Western heritage, and how they correspond with some basic human responses to life and to ourselves. The third part of the book addresses how we begin to enter into a process of healing, wholeness and inner reconciliation with ourselves, particularly after we have been in council with some of our more difficult dragons. The final part of the book is dedicated to the practical steps we can take in learning how to tame our dragons and include them as vital elements of inner healing and reconciliation process that we must all go through when engaged in a process of inner growth. This is the work (*praxis*) of dragon-taming.

Our dragons allow us to complete the circle of inner healing and transformation, which must include all of the elements of joy, brokenness, creativity, and transformation. Our exploration about dragons in this book will be guided by the principles of radical curiosity and acceptance, as we begin the process of re-training our Western minds to develop a different relationship with our dragons. This circle of healing and transformation calls upon us to cultivate a willingness to enter into *The Fire That Never Dies*, which is an eternal flame that cleanses and burns away that which no longer brings us sustained joy, life, and an ability to connect meaningfully with ourselves and with others.

The Fire That Never Dies

Inside a warm, secluded cave (or is it a room?) sits an old man
Some call him wise
Some call him "sick with experience"
He calls himself nothing, but he sits with everything
He sits in front of a fire that never dies
For thousands of years, he has contemplated how he might be able to one day
Touch the fire without getting burned
He has tried many times, with no success

Some days he grows young with ambition
And other days he grows old with despair
He has many stories to tell
He is not the same as the ambition
He is not the same as the despair
Such things are stories that are merely told through him
For, if he would call himself anything, it would be

Vessel
But even vessels get curious…

And once again, the old man contemplates
How he might touch the fire without getting burned
He tells long tales to anyone who would sit and listen
Some tales last a hundred years
Some, a thousand
And still some, longer yet…

In between tales, his thoughts always return to the fire
The fire that never dies
Aching, as he is, to reach out and touch the flames

He can hold the vibrancy of youth, but has moved beyond its rashness
He knows how to sit still and wait
He has learned that, in his stillness
Things will come to him
Sometimes in fragments, and every so often as a whole
And in his stillness one day, a thought occurs to him
How he can boil love down into a single idea
A molecule
A fine point, at the center of all gravity, called "compassion"
Passion, *com*-pressed

He knows
He has awareness
He has carnal knowledge
He cannot return to his innocence
The way back is shut

Compassion, he learns, is not possible without consciousness
It is a singular idea
And yet forever stretching out
In greater complexity and synthesis
Contained in one fine element

An eternal flame…

He knows
He has awareness
He understands that he is to give himself over to the fire
His life will spread with the ashes
His essence, his being, his passion and presence
Compressed into one fine molecule
Until it explodes
And he, with it
His remnants scatter far and abroad
His dust, the universe
His children, the scattered and growing fire

His awareness expands, his compassion, awake
And he is open
He is the fire

And he is not alone…

He perceives a She
She is He
He is She
She has been stirring He awake
Injecting him with hopeless curiosity
She will create
She will weave back together what has been scattered
She will give birth to the fire that awakens in everyone
She will bring back together what has been lost
She will teach He again and again, how to surrender to the fire
By making love

Expand, contract
Up, down
Birth, death
And birth again
Awake, asleep
Awake…
AWAKE!

Part I

Where Our Dragons Are Born

"How could we forget those ancient myths that are at the beginning of all peoples, the myths about dragons that at the last moment turn into princesses? Perhaps all the dragons in our lives are princesses who are only waiting to see us act, just once, with beauty and courage. Perhaps everything that frightens us is, in its deepest essence, something helpless that wants our love."

~Rainer Maria Rilke[i]

Chapter 1
Dragons, Fire and the Power of Myth

Myths provide us with soul nourishment. The stories of myth form the undercurrent of our lives. Joseph Campbell, Marie Louise von Franz, Rollo May, and Carl Jung were among some of the first Western scholars to reawaken the modern world to the importance and function of myth. Contrary to our modern interpretation of a myth as being nothing more than a tall tale or a false narrative, myths instead reveal to us the deeper, abiding truths of human nature and existence. They give us wisdom and insight into ourselves, and they tell the story of our species, letting us know both, where we come from and where we are going.

In this sense, myths are not static stories, stuck in a lonely moment of time. Rather, they are living entities. They evolve with us and we evolve with them. The stories of who we are and where we come from are also the stories of where we are going and what we are about to become. Joseph Campbell teaches us that it is "the prime function of mythology and rite to supply the symbols that carry the human spirit forward…"[ii]

Our myths are our birthrights. Part of our job in becoming human is to reconnect with our own myths and begin to consciously live the stories that they are telling through us. While we have collective myths that inform us of our heritage and the nature of our relationships, myth also speaks to the internal reality and landscape of the individual human being, or human psyche. Myths provide us with an opportunity to recognize different parts of ourselves being expressed through all of the diverse characters and creatures within its stories, revealing timeless, recurring themes that we all recognize intuitively. A myth invites us into a direct experience of human life, mirroring back to us our own stories about ourselves. A myth is a story that is able to capture our own projections and feed them back to us in a way that is more palatable for us to see, accept, and understand. When we read the great myths, we are reading the ancient blueprints of our souls. Myths communicate to us our strongest hopes and desires as well as our deepest and most abiding fears.

Myths hold a power over us that we cannot deny or explain away. They are an underlying, guiding presence in all of our lives, whether we are aware of it or not. The myth provides nourishment for us, and while our myths do not always answer all of our questions about life, they do inspire us to perhaps begin asking better questions. They also encourage us to learn how to simply live with their images and symbols consciously, without always having to fully understand them first.

The characters and creatures of myth, whether good, evil or complex admixtures of both, are repeating our stories back to us in dramatic form. Naturally, when we read these stories, we find certain characters that we like and are drawn to, while others we find repugnant. Our job, when reading a story mythologically, is to see parts of ourselves in *all* of its characters, not just the ones we like. Myths reveal to us that we are all on a quest. Our natural curiosity carries a certain naiveté that allows us the freedom to explore the unknown without becoming paralyzed by our fear of it.

Myths serve a social function as well. They guide how we form communities and relationships around shared values, ethics, and moral codes. They teach us about what we have chosen to love and what we have chosen to hate; what we have chosen to value and what we have chosen to discard. Our myths teach us about our biases and prejudices and how we choose to sustain or reject them over time. Myths reveal to us a collective identity, whether that identify be informed by a family, a tribe, a community, a nation-state, or a religion. Myths provide us with powerful symbols and rites to reinforce our values, while at the same time providing us with clues about which of our old values are meant to be abandoned and new values that must learn to be embraced and lived.

It is to our own detriment that we remain unaware of our own myths, for in doing so, we remain unconscious of our own guiding principles. Myths become dangerous when we act them out unconsciously. They need our full, conscious participation in order for them to stay alive, healthy and imbued with life-giving purpose. While myths do hold enduring truths, they also have a malleability with which they adjust to new paradigms that are being born in the world through us as we continue to grow and mature as a species. While myths reveal the enduring truths and stories of our shared humanity, they also move, grow and evolve along with us. Myths are living stories. They require our ability to be flexible and change when new knowledge and new paradigms come into our awareness.

When we ignore our own myths, the result is that they tend to denigrate into dogmatic beliefs, rituals, routines, and interpretations of truth. They grow stale and boring, and in the process become more rigid and inflexible.

Fundamentalism is the inevitable result of a myth gone dormant in the imagination of those who have lost the ability to stay connected to their own living stories and history. It is the graveyard for a living myth that has been allowed to die. Living myths are meant to guide us through different stages of our own growth and evolution as a human species, not keep us stunted and stuck.

Myths provide us with symbols and rites that are designed to help us move forward with our own growth and evolution. Symbols are powerful representations of the beliefs we hold dear, born and cultivated by our ancestors as their stories are passed from one generation to the next. Each character or creature of myth, as a representation of some part of our psyches, can be a symbol that provides us meaning, strength, and even courage when we need it. These symbols support and give us strength, particularly when we find ourselves wandering into new and unknown territory in our lives. Rather than encouraging us to retreat back into what is familiar, powerful symbols encourage us to be brave and move forward, even though we do not always know what lies ahead of us.

The Fire That Never Dies is a symbol I have chosen for this book and the subject of dragons. It is a powerful symbol reminding us of the never-ending cycles of birth, death and rebirth. It is true that we shall all one day perish from the Earth. It is also true that we are meant to experience many smaller deaths and rebirths along the way, throughout our lifetimes. This eternal Fire is a symbol that teaches us how to surrender ourselves to all of the little deaths we must face in our lives in order for new life to be born within us.

The Fire itself holds a great paradoxical tension between being a force of both destruction and rebirth. It is a fire of transformation and growth. It is designed to help us burn away old stories of ourselves that no longer serve us well and must be cleared away in order to give birth to the new stories trying to emerge from within us. When we let go of all that is no longer necessary for our own growth and healing, to make room for new life and new stories, we emerge from that process stronger, wiser, kinder, gentler and more compassionate; bolder and more self-assured. Another great symbol of this eternal truth about the cycles of death and rebirth is the great Phoenix that burns to ashes when it dies and is then reborn from them anew.

Knowing about the nature of this Fire does not mean we cease to fear it. We fear it greatly and we do everything we can to avoid it. We know that we are going to have to give up something by walking through those flames. The Fire threatens our internal status quo. It threatens to rid us of old stories of ourselves that, even if they no longer serve us or may even be harming us, we are reluctant to let go of, if for no other reason than they are familiar. Our fears of the unknown can overwhelm all other senses. This truth is what has helped to spurn the phrase, "I'd rather stick with the devil I know, than risk the devil I don't know." Our instinct is to protect our stories, whether they are giving us life or draining us of it, with the same vigor we protect ourselves from outward harm. We do not give up easily what we believe belongs to us, and we hold tightly to our own stories and understanding of who we are. It is natural for us to feel reluctant and to hesitate before we allow ourselves to consider undergoing the cleansing process of the eternal fire. This hesitance may actually save us from a temptation toward hubris when approaching those flames, for if we try to transgress them without humility, we run the very real risk of burning ourselves up and burning ourselves out.

Eventually, however, resistance must give way to resolve, and hubris must give way to humility. We cannot stay stuck forever. The Fire reminds us of the impermanence of all things, and the continuous cycles of birth, death, and rebirth. The Fire will be patient with us for a time, but not forever. If we find ourselves resisting it for too long, the Fire will reach out to us in the form of a Dragon to grab our attention and get us moving. The Dragon is that creature of myth that does not allow us to stay stagnate or let our myths deteriorate into dogmas and empty rituals of personal piety. These are forms of avoidance and resistance to our souls' true purpose. Somewhere, deep down within us, we know that we cannot stay in one place for too long. We both, long for and fear, the presence of this eternal Fire, always burning, waiting for us to approach it in different moments in our lives. When we find ourselves naked and exposed to our deepest fears and strongest desires in conflict with each other, there we find ourselves face to face with a dragon.

Dragons are real. And they're all in our head…

Our dragons bring with them knowledge and awareness of the rich depth and complexity of our own nature. They bear wisdom and insight, alerting us to the presence of unsuspected and unsought treasure that lies beneath our old wounds and brokenness. To receive these gifts and treasures, however, we must first learn to tolerate the presence of our own dragons, for they are the great guardians of the unknown treasures of our soul. We must learn to speak with them, listen to them and allow them to play the role that they are meant to play, to instigate the healing process of our own inner fragmentation.

Because most of us have spent the majority of our lives cultivating good defense mechanisms in our waking lives, we are less likely to acknowledge our dragons when we are awake. The only exception to this rule is when we find ourselves in great pain or suffering, during which we find ourselves exposed to more of our vulnerability than we feel capable of handling under normal circumstances. For this reason, we are far more likely to hear from our dragons in dreams, visions and rare, unguarded moments in our waking lives.

Before we proceed further with how our subconscious connects us to our dragons, a quick word about pain and suffering is needed. Throughout this book we will be exploring moments of suffering and the potential gifts we stand to receive in the midst of it. It is important, however, to make a clear distinction between pain and suffering that promotes personal growth and potential healing, and pain that is willful and destructive. Any redemptive qualities of suffering that may be addressed in this book should not be confused with any forms of masochism, abuse, torture, rape, terrorism, misogyny, racism, sexism, xenophobia, homophobia or any other forms of exclusivity. Pain for the sake of pain is not redemptive and none of us has a right to willfully inflict pain on anyone for any reason. These forms of pain are intended to exert cruel power and domination over others and are injurious not only to our lives, but our very souls. These forms of pain are what I would readily designate as "evil," and evil is never to be tolerated or propagated.

The kind of pain that is designed to wake us up and get us moving has more to do with the pain of discomfort and the loss of something that one has been holding onto for dear life, preventing one's own personal healing and growth. We are not meant to stay in one place in our lives for very long. We are meant to keep moving. I like the phrase, "stop and smell the roses," because it encourages us to slow down and enjoy life as it is. I would add an addendum to that, however, which would be "…but don't linger too long." We are not meant to stay stuck on any one "rose" as it were, and in order for us to be able to move forward and explore more of the roses we are destined to discover, we must be able to experience the discomfort necessary to find our motivation to leave our familiar roses behind and go looking for new ones.

Pain does have the effect of jolting us awake, whether we are feeling the tugs of our own growing pangs, in the midst of deep grief and loss, or victimized by evil forms of pain. The only redemptive part of those moments is our ability to choose to heal ourselves and continue to grow, even in spite of terrible things that have happened to us. Pain does force us to change, not because we choose to, but because we are often left with no other choice. The world has changed for us and we must change with it. Pain always initiates a journey. This is not a journey we may have chosen, but we are now faced with the choice to take it or not.

When our defenses are down, the veil between our conscious lives, and all of the material that resides in our unconscious lives, becomes thin. We already experience this reality in our dreams. Our dragons present themselves in our dreams and visions. Dragons also present themselves in our projections.

Almost all of our distasteful and uncomfortable encounters with other people include a projection of some sort. These projections are rejected parts of ourselves that we have relegated to our unconsciousness. They only manifest consciously in the form of projection and these projections attach themselves to other people that trigger that awareness inside of us just by their mere presence in our lives.

Our dragons will also begin to appear in our lives when we are getting ready for important life transitions. If we start to drag our feet for too long when faced with significant transitions, our dragons arrive to jolt us out of our stupor. Our dragons bring us face to face with our own internal resistances and force us to deal with them. In order for us to move through our own resistances, we must first be able to acknowledge that they exist. We avoid acknowledging them because we know that where we find a resistance, we are going to find a dragon there to push us into it and into the eternal Fire.

If we have not learned how to parley with our dragons, our confrontation with them at the crossroads of our own resistances will become treacherous. Dragons require our deepest respect. They do not suffer our ignorance or arrogance well. They are not to be offended or dismissed lightly, and they have no tolerance for our excuses. They must always be approached with great care, wisdom, and above all, humility. If we choose to face our dragons with anything but these things, our dragons will consume us. If, however, we choose to learn the language of our dragons and agree to treat them with care and respect, then we will become recipients of their great wisdom and power. When we allow ourselves to recognize a dragon as an aspect of our own psyches, imbued with purpose, it allows us to lessen our guard a little to accept and befriend it. When our dragon feels safe enough to become our ally, only then do we have access to its great power and vitality, choosing to use these things wisely in our lives.

Our dragons remind us, however disruptively, that we are not meant to sit idly while our lives pass us by. As humans, we are creatures of purpose and meaning. Both require an ability for movement on our part, and our dragons will appear to us when we have become too complacent in our lives. As we learn the art of taming and befriending our dragons, we also learn to expose ourselves to our strongest desires and deepest fears and do not allow our internal resistances to distract us from the task of acknowledging and accepting them. It is only when we greet our fears and learn to no longer fear them that we create a life-giving alliance with our dragons.

When we accept and value our own dragons, they cease to be our antagonists. They switch their allegiance from adversary to ally. They will protect and defend us as long as we take care of them and do not offend them.

This encourages us to continue to remain wise and cautious with our dragons, for they will quickly revert back to becoming our antagonist again if we attempt to abuse or misuse the power and vitality that they have to offer us.

We must learn to tame and befriend our own personal dragons if we have any hope of learning how to tame our collective ones. We are living in a time in our history where the survival of our species may depend on our ability to do this kind of work. We are intended to be gifts to our world, but if we cannot do our own work, we can quickly become our own worst enemies. The recognition of the gifts our dragons have to bring, as well as our ability to accept them, reveals to us an enduring truth that we are much more than we ever think we are or can be. We avoid taking responsibility for this truth because it does require a lot from us. For us to claim our birthrights, however, we must be willing to do our work. The result is that we become agents of greater wisdom, compassion, and purpose in this world, which in turn encourages others to do the same. When we embody these principles, we become vessels of joy and healing, not only for ourselves but for the world around us.

Dragons can be fierce lovers and protectors. In order for us to learn this truth about our dragons, however, we must deal with a long history of projected antagonism, evil, greed, and hatred imbued in our Western myths regarding dragons. As we shall see, this characterization of dragons is not consistent in other places around the world, primarily in Asian myths that bear a very different relationship with dragons, and dragon-taming. It will become our task to first become familiar with our own dragons before we can begin to ask the question of how we learn to tame them.

Chapter 2
The Dragon Archetype and the
Western World

Carl Jung had a word for mythological motifs that are universal, appearing in one form or another across all cultures and myths. This, he called the *archetype*, and a dragon is an archetypal creature of myth and legend, the likes of which can be found across all cultures and civilizations around the world in different forms. Dragons can symbolize many different things depending on where they come from and what purpose they serve. Some dragons are capable of flight, armed with monstrous wings. Other dragons slither across the land or swim through the dark depths of the seas. Some dragons breathe fire while others spew water. Some dragons are capable of killing you by simply looking into their eyes while other dragons may be completely blind. One thing that all dragons have in common is that they are very powerful and capable of causing a lot of trouble.

Dragons inspire in us a healthy respect and a numinous awe. Only the foolhardy dare tempt fate by provoking a dragon's wrath willingly. Dragons, bearing such power in our imaginations, weave their way through many of our own stories, myths and legends. They spring from the depths of our souls to ignite a fire we never knew was there, but now must contend and come to terms with, until we learn to tame and embrace it.

When archetypal creatures and images appear in our dreams and in our great myths, we are wise to pay attention, for something powerful is stirring in the underworld of our psyches, which is about to break forth into our very consciousness. Archetypal images often provoke us into a journey of discovery. These journeys of the soul guide us into the dark corners and unexplored regions of ourselves. The undiscovered country, as it turns out, "at whose sight the happy smile, and the accursed damn'd,"[iii] is primarily an inner quest of the soul.

Joseph Campbell writes, "The passage of the mythological hero may be over ground, incidentally; fundamentally it is inward—into depths where obscure resistances are overcome, and long-lost forgotten powers are revivified, to be made available for the transfiguration of the world."[iv]

While a sense of adventure and excitement can help us to instigate these journeys into worlds and realms, we yet know nothing about, they always bring us to the places unexpected and unsought. Often times, a quest begins with a reluctant hero; one who finds her or himself face to face with a journey they did not choose but must embark on regardless. Often, we find ourselves thrust into a journey at a moment of crisis or suffering, and often unprepared. Regardless of what pushed us out the door of the safety and comfort of that which is familiar to us—whether we are inspired by excitement or urgency to proceed further—it is guaranteed that somewhere along the trail we will encounter the goblins, dragons, trolls, specters, demons, and monsters we would rather avoid. What we do in these moments may spell the difference between our ability to survive and thrive, or not. Our ability to greet these creatures wisely will determine our fate.

As stated in the previous chapter, the myths and legends we have inherited from our own ancestors play a large role in determining what we do and how we behave in moments like this. While different cultures have different dragons, one of the most striking differences we observe is between the dragons of Eastern myth and legend, and its Western counterparts. In our Western myths, dragons almost always symbolize forms of evil that must be resisted and conquered in order for the world to be made right again. In Eastern myths, there is more room for dragons that carry a wisdom and regality to them that is meant to benefit us in some way. Sometimes these dragons are guides and protectors. Some dragons are large enough to carry the entire world beneath their large, hooded heads, as a great serpent. Doug Niles writes, "Although the dragons of East Asian culture are powerful and capable of doing a great deal of damage, they are generally not regarded as the greedy, destructive, and wicked wyrms that are featured in European myths. Many tales of Asian dragons show the serpents helping humankind."[v]

While I believe it is wise for us to learn how other cultures and cultural myths deal with their own dragons, ultimately, I believe it to be folly for us to simply imitate their methods. There are some fundamental differences between the Eastern Psyche and the Western Psyche that do not necessarily allow us to simply borrow one from the other, at least not without great thought, care and perseverance to remain aware of our own fundamental biases about human nature, depending on where we grew up.

One of the more striking differences between Eastern and Western myths regarding our human nature is the concept of the importance of the individual, in contrast to that of the collective experience. Our recognition of an individual

Ego in Western cultures and traditions, as autonomously distinct from all other individuals and forms of life, is fundamentally different from an Eastern understanding of an individual as belonging to a larger, collective consciousness, where all things are connected in a particular way. This is neither good nor bad, it is just different. As folks who are born and raised in Western traditions, we experience a duality to the world that is not necessarily experienced by those raised in societies that value the collective experience of the human Psyche over the individual one.

This fundamental difference, in the way that the Eastern archetypal human being and the Western archetypal human being experience the world of the Self, appears to be a fundamental one that cannot simply be removed, even by choice. For better and worse, this experience of ourselves as separate, individual entities as Western people gives us a very different template from which to approach our relationship with dragons than it would in Eastern cultures. It is wise for us to respect that difference and always tell the truth about ourselves, for if we fail to do this, we fail to comprehend our own paths toward healing and wholeness that may be very different from others.

Because we carry with us, as Western people, this sense of duality, we are more prone to experiencing ourselves and the world around us as being fragmented, and this is one of the consequences of apprehending our world through the experience of the individual ego. From this experience of inner duality, we experience the tension of opposites, and those opposites are often in conflict with each other. Our task as Western people is not to learn how to resolve the tension of opposites by their dissolution, so much as it is to learn how to reconcile opposites and balance the paradoxical tensions they present to us. These paradoxical tensions, like dragons, force us to pay attention, particularly when our instinct is to try to resolve those tensions too quickly, which as we shall see in the next chapter, is not always helpful in our quest to befriend our own dragons.

It is our task, as Western people, to learn how to tame and befriend dragons on our own terms, using our own tools, and our own language. We are living in a time right now where the world desperately needs us to learn how to do our own work. I believe our avoidance and even abandonment of the need for our own inner reconciliation process is causing great suffering in the world. Our resistance to learn something new about our dragons and about ourselves that might allow us to make the paradigm shifts, I believe are necessary at this time in our history, is only serving to fragment us even further. This is but one of the many reasons why it is so important for us to work with our own myths. Not simply to understand where they come from, but also to understand where they are taking us, and how they may be getting us ready for transformation.

One of the enduring modern myths we hold dear as Western individuals is the mythology of the "Wild West." These myths tell us stories of courage, bravery, ingenuity, and resourcefulness. They are stories of independence and resilience, and these are things that we deeply admire and value. Accompanying these stories is a strong impulse to embody the values of will-power and determination. With these tools, we can create and accomplish great things. We can create great legacies and produce incredible technology. It is the myth of *rugged individualism*, particularly within North American mythologies, that has informed us of our identity and the values we hold true.

The stories of the Wild West, with their mythic heroes like John Wayne and Clint Eastwood, reflect a strong desire for a singular autonomy, untethered and free to explore and create itself. The value of the rugged individual, reflected in these stories, invites us to consider what we may be capable of when we have no restraints imposed upon us. It also brings with it its own blind spots, however, as do all individual values alone and unto themselves. What these myths of rugged individualism often fail to acknowledge is the existence of their own shadows.

These kinds of myths rely heavily on a solid, dualistic understanding of human nature, with clear delineations between black and white, right and wrong, and good guys vs. bad guys. Hence, these mythic motifs rely on a simple and uncomplicated understanding of the nature of good and evil. Good guys can only do good and bad guys can only do bad. Because of this, bad guys must always be stopped, and if necessary, killed. If one considers oneself to be a good guy, not much more thought needs to be put into one's actions, as the underlying assumption is that they are always good and come from a place of always wanting to do good, even if what that person has to do is harm someone else to accomplish the good. This same value arises when one speaks of the pursuit of happiness, often confused in our modern world, with the accumulation of wealth. A moral imperative that arises in this overstated dualism is that if someone threatens your ambition or challenges your values in any way, you simply get rid of them.

The mythos of rugged individualism has a very difficult time tolerating the idea that an action, especially the act of one of the good guys, is capable of producing both virtue *and* harm. It bristles at being called to account for its actions and resists any admonition that its judgment could be compromised or incomplete in some way. It cannot acknowledge its own blind spots because it cannot accept that it has any. In the Wild West mythos, it becomes necessary to have bad guys to fight, because much of the purpose of a good guy is centered around his ability to defeat the bad guy. In the mythos of the Wild West, the dragon must always represent that evil which is to be conquered. In other words, the existence of a dragon is necessary to keep the dragon-slayer employed. As well, it needs the dragon to project all of its own unrecognized darkness onto it. Whatever we might detest about ourselves will be projected onto our own dragons which must then be slain.

Because the myths of rugged individualism neglect the existence of their own shadows, they fail to explore the regions of their own darkness and the possibility that they too, are capable of committing acts of evil. In this strict binary there is little to no need for inner reflection, and so these myths fail to help us understand that much of which we determine to be "evil" is only a projection of our own fears, hatred and greed onto whatever enemy we create to embody that evil potential for us. The mythos of the Wild West fails to perceive the plight of our enemy as our own. The myth of rugged individualism, while very attractive to us, also carries a lonely solipsism that has a tendency to steer us away from participating in genuine community, with all of the complexities, imperfections and responsibilities that this brings. Belonging to a genuine community includes having an ability to sacrifice something for the greater common good, which is not a value that the rugged individualist can embrace.

The denial of the human shadow in myths of rugged individualism ultimately leads to an imbalance in our psyches that can manifest as a destructive entitlement. It becomes very easy for us to believe that we have an inherent right to every resource the earth provides, including a right to take these resources by force, if needs be.

There was a time when the world was a much bigger place, where this mythos perhaps made a lot more sense, and may have indeed been a necessary step in our evolution as a human species, but now the world is much, much smaller. We now have an awareness that our earth's resources are not infinite. We now have an awareness that our habits of consumption as human beings have a direct consequence on all others around us. We can no longer pretend that our every action does not have either a direct or indirect impact on all others that we share this planet with. We live in a global society and are interdependent with each other more than we have ever been in our own history.

The myths of the Wild West are not new as much as they are new forms of an old story that runs through our history as Western people. We need an awareness of our old myths in order to be able to allow them to transform alongside us as we grow and change, ever adapting to new paradigms, the likes of which are always inevitable. We need to engage our myths as living entities, and do so consciously, for we are living out those myths all the time whether we are aware of them or not.

Without our conscious, willing participation, our myths act out unconsciously and can become very destructive. The myth requires our ability to read ourselves into it as it is reading itself into us, one of many paradoxical tensions that this book will begin to address. We are in a symbiotic relationship with our own myths, which can take on a life of their own if we remain unconscious of them. When we fully and consciously interact with them, we bring them to life in very powerful and important ways. When we do this, we fulfill one of the great purposes of our lives. When we do this, we learn about the different parts of ourselves and how they seek expression in our daily lives, including our own dragons.

It is time for us to learn how to embrace a larger view of our dragons, which is to say that it is time for us to embrace a larger view of ourselves. The purpose of this book is to create a road map for us, as Western people, to learn how to acknowledge, engage, and befriend our dragons. I dare risk the hypothesis that our myths about dragons have grown stale and risk falling into forms of dogma and empty piety, rather than promoting the growth and evolution of our species. It is time for us to learn that not all dragons are meant to be slain, and that if we insist on continuing this dogmatic narrative about them, it is to our detriment and possible doom. We have slowly been killing off our natural curiosity in favor of institutions designed to quantify data about us rather than help us to more deeply explore and understand ourselves and where we come from. We are turning ourselves into cattle as we are continually taught to deny ourselves the work of our inner lives. In some cases, we are even being told that there is no such thing as an inner life.

We need to resurrect the healing art of curiosity once more, and in doing so, must become more curious and aware of our own myths, and all of the assumptions of our own nature being carried by those myths. When we enact those assumptions unconsciously, we end up inflicting great harm upon ourselves and upon others. We risk brutally imposing our values on others who do not share those assumptions and beliefs, as though doing so is a perpetration of virtue rather than an act of evil.

Our dragons are but one manifestation of all that beckons us to explore our myths and the symbols they carry, for as we learn to explore our own myths, we learn to explore our own souls. We must allow ourselves to investigate every aspect of our own individual and collective psyches, including its dark and shadowy places. As a light-centric society, we no longer have any good, collective rites, and rituals to learn how to investigate our shadows safely and wisely. We must learn a different kind of courage, one which we are not accustomed to. It is not the courage of the dragon-slayer, but the courage of the dragon-tamer that we are now being called to cultivate. We must understand that the presence of the dragon is a manifestation of ourselves. As soon as the dragon-slayer is able to see himself as the dragon, he can then change his vocation in life to dragon-tamer.

Not all that arises out of the darkness of our psyches is evil or harmful, but these things will become so if we continue to neglect or fight them. We cannot conquer our own human shadows any more than we can conquer the dragons that produce them. Our task is to learn how to explore our shadows, for there lie the roots of our inner fragmentation. There also lie the roots for our inner healing and reconciliation as well.

Once awareness is born within us, it cannot be unborn. Once we discover the existence of our own dragons, we can no longer claim innocence of them. Our growing awareness of ourselves exposes us to all of the places within us where we are at war with ourselves. It exposes the many tensions and unresolved fears that we carry every day. Consciousness exposes us to the knowledge of paradoxical tensions we must learn to balance, as the tension of opposites produces the possibility of something creative at work within us, awakening us to the possibilities of new life.

Chapter 3
The Tensions of the Paradox

As individual people, we are made up of many different elements and aspects of our inner psyches, all looking to express themselves in our lives and to be regarded with dignity and respect. We are beautifully, and at times frustratingly, complex and multi-faceted creatures. We experience both inner harmony and inner discord. We are capable of both loving and hating ourselves, as we are capable of loving and hating each other. We can experience peace and contentment, as well as fear and shame. We experience both joy and despair. We are capable of extraordinary acts of kindness, self-sacrifice and courage, as well as monstrous acts of violence, war, and terror. We experience both inner unity and inner fragmentation.

These paradoxical tensions are evidence of the many different aspects of our human nature, expressing themselves in different ways. They are attached to different stories we tell about ourselves as well as the stories that have been handed down to us from others, both for good and for ill. Each of these stories are looking to express themselves in different ways throughout our lives. All our inner stories and the parts of our personality that embody them are important for us to learn about, because they are influencing us whether we are aware of them or not. It is important that we listen to them and learn to care for them properly.

In every community, there is the tension that exists between those who think and feel one way about something, and those who think and feel another way. The same is true of our inner "community" as well. Different parts of our personalities are designed to take care of and respond to different things. They are all important but are likely to be at odds with each other from time to time. Most of the time, they operate unseen, beyond our awareness, even as they regularly influence our daily thoughts, actions, biases, prejudices, attitudes, and choices. For the most part, we remain unaware of many of these parts of us until they get disturbed in some way or ignored for too long. Then these parts begin to stir up and disrupt our delicate internal balancing acts as they work hard to get our attention.

As we grow and learn about ourselves, we also come to learn more about the different parts of our psyches and what they do. Many of these parts are pleasant to experience as well as discover within us, like learning that there is an inner artist waiting to come out that we never knew was in there before or being surprised to learn that one is good at acting, even though one experiences stage fright. These parts of ourselves that we greet warmly and generate internal strength and courage from, we generally regard as our inner *allies*. We like them, and they help us out in some way. Then there are those parts of us that we have grown to fear or hate, and we often either wage war on, or push further into our shadows in our attempts to ignore them, hoping that they will just eventually disappear. More frightening to us are parts of ourselves that come from these places that we had no idea even existed inside of us at all. Typically, we only become aware of these parts when they get triggered by unique encounters and circumstances. These parts, at least initially, we are likely to regard as our *dragons*.

There are other parts that we may regard indifferently, but we do not tend to think of those parts as antagonists because they are not particularly troubling to us. They are no less important, but they tend not to get our attention very often. The parts that get our attention the most enhance the fundamental feeling-principle of duality, I have argued is common to all of us in the West. It is our job to learn how to balance the tension between our allies and our dragons, greet each of them with curiosity, and discern what they are here to teach us. How we choose to greet all our inner characters matters a great deal. If we treat them as enemies, then we can expect them to behave as enemies. Conversely, if we can greet them as friends or potential allies, then they are more likely to respond in kind.

Transformative growth is a continual process of the recognition and acceptance of the wholeness to which we come from and are returning to, now with consciousness. It is the necessary journey out of innocence and into awareness. The inevitable tensions we feel during the growing process are a part of what fuels the engines of growth. The opposites, we discover, are not always intended for *opposition*. That is dualism. A paradoxical tension is different from a dualism. A dualism seeks no relationship or resolution. A dualism signifies an essential opposition or antagonism, whereas a paradoxical tension seeks a dialogue and where necessary, a reconciliation. Balancing the tension helps to hold us in check so that we do not become consumed or possessed by any one part of our psyches. It is what allows us to begin, to bring reconciliation between the parts of ourselves that do feel antagonistic toward each other.

Because the balancing of opposites helps to promote creativity and growth, we learn to endure the tension of the paradox before rushing in too quickly to resolve it. We learn that the masculine needs the feminine, light needs the dark, joy is often mixed with grief, and so on. Because these opposites are difficult to balance, our instinct is to label some of them as being "good" and others "bad." While I do not deny the existence of both good and evil in the world, I assert that many things that we label as being good or bad have more to do with our comfort or discomfort with them than they do, necessarily with being morally righteous or corrupt. There are far more instances when utilizing these two value judgments prohibit us from exploring further, learning more, and growing up, because they provide escape routes out of the fear and anxiety we are experiencing in the tension. The tension can, at times, feel so uncomfortable or so threatening to our understanding of ourselves, that we are often tempted to confuse this tension with psychological pathology or perhaps, even evil itself. Naturally, when we label something as evil, we are less inclined to want to become curious about it.

If we do not practice balancing the opposites, we will predictably become unbalanced. This happens to us as individual people and collectively as communities. Our modern, Western world has been operating too long in an unbalanced state. We must allow ourselves the curiosity necessary to explore all the reasons for this. It will require us to consider all the places we have been taught either to avoid or attack, both inside and outside of ourselves. It will require an ability to look at, and possibly reassess, some of those beliefs, traditions, and ways of thinking that have become sacred to us in some way, but no longer make sense if we are to continue the journey forward. It is in these places that we also find the keys for our own healing and growth as we learn to accept and embrace greater levels of awareness and wisdom. We will not be able to heal either our individual or our collective wounds until we learn to walk these seemingly treacherous paths into our own shadows.

This kind of journey then, that we are being called to take, is indicative of the mythical motif of the *hero*. As Joseph Campbell writes, "The hero, whether god or goddess…discovers and assimilates 'their' opposite (unsuspected self) either by swallowing it or being swallowed. One by one, the resistances are broken."[vi] When we discover that these opposite energies within us are not meant to be at war with each other, we learn how to let them work together, and we let go of our need to fight ourselves. When we learn how to balance the forces which are presented to us as opposites, we learn that they belong to each other in a way that brings both wisdom and vitality. New life comes from the kinds of struggles that provoke us to learn how to balance these tensions within us, and we must learn how to both enter and exit these struggles appropriately. Our dragons are the faces of our own fears and insecurities, as well as our own untapped potential. Until we learn to stop fighting and embrace them, we choose to be at continual war with ourselves.

A guiding principle that I believe must be practiced in order to successfully learn the art of dragon-taming is curiosity. *Curiosity is the antidote to shame and fear.* Attachment to shame and fear are what keep old stories and old ways of dealing with pain alive inside of us long after they were meant to die. Old ways of coping that were birthed many years ago, and which made sense to us at the time as a way to survive, will require our ability to grieve the loss of when it is time to say goodbye to them, especially if they have now become a hindrance to our growth. We *will* need to grieve their loss, even though they have been causing us pain. We cannot heal our wounds until we grieve them, and to grieve them we first must be able to acknowledge and experience them. One cannot let go of what one cannot first acknowledge. Our curiosity can teach us compassion for ourselves in these vulnerable moments.

The balancing of opposites is crucial to our growth. It is not only an acknowledgment of our experience of inner fragmentation, but it provides a potential source of energy to get us moving along our own journeys of growth. This cannot happen in a state of innocence, where we remain unaware of these inner tensions. This is why developing our consciousness and engaging the individuation process is so important. The problem is that we have confused this experience of a divided, or broken state of being, with a fixed and broken human nature. We have tricked ourselves into believing that a state of duality *is* our nature, rather than a particular journey that has been placed before us to walk through on our way back into wholeness, a journey which most of us remain unaware of. Because we believe that this inner fragmentation is our original nature and state, we ironically make ourselves less aware of it, and more prone toward acting this drama out unconsciously rather than purposefully. Inner fragmentation is not our original state, but it is a path that must break us open to the need to instigate a journey into consciousness.

This is a difficult state that many of us have found ourselves in, unsure of how to re-discover this mythical wholeness that we all come from, and in truth, having abandoned the idea that there is any such original unity in the first place. In practice, what we are really trying to do is return to our innocence, which is why we continue to feel despair, when in actuality, what we are returning to is an awareness of this underlying wholeness with consciousness and purpose. Our experience of inner fragmentation is the vehicle that propels us out of innocence and into the world of conscious awareness. The experience of inner fragmentation is why we are all destined to have a confrontation with the rejected parts of our psyches that we have relegated to our own shadows. This is why dragons are birthed into existence. They are the heralds of an important journey ahead and the torch-bearers of insight and recognition of the unexplored opposite functions of our ego-ideals, that we need to greet with awareness and curiosity, so that the work of reconciliation is made possible.

Balancing a paradox without rushing in to resolve it right away can be difficult because it is very uncomfortable. This, however, brings me to my next guiding principle; *difficulty is not pathology.* In other words, just because we find something to be difficult does not mean that there is something wrong with us or that we are incapable. It simply means that it is difficult. The high achievers and perfectionists among us (myself included) will have the hardest time accepting this principle. We do not feel quite at ease unless we can take some measure of personal responsibility for making our various tasks in life difficult. However, when we recognize that the experience of difficulty itself is not evidence of personal pathology, we begin to experience grace above shame, for we are not stuck beating ourselves up for finding some of our tasks in life to be hard.

A difficult task is enough for us to have to contend without any additional shame or harsh self-judgment we may be tempted to contribute to it. In fact, the very realization that we are encountering something difficult may be an indication that we are doing something right, for we have allowed ourselves to greet a resistance, and when we greet a resistance, we are knocking on the door to the next challenge and corresponding level of wisdom we are meant to encounter. A resistance can be an indication that we are ready to receive what is next on our journeys of growth. It means that we are no longer willing to stay stuck and that it is time for us to get moving. Something in our soul, that vast reservoir of collected wisdom and knowledge, decided that we were ready to take on the next task, so it provoked the right resistance at the right time to provide us with the experience of walking through that resistance and into deeper levels of wisdom and joy.

Growing pangs are seldom fun to experience but are in fact necessary for our growth. They are an indication that something important is happening and that things are moving. They push us out of our comfort zones enough so that we begin to pay attention to the new things meant for us to learn. If we resist too much, or try to escape our task by retreating back into unconsciousness, then a dragon appears to wake us up and grab our attention. When we learn to embrace the process of acknowledging our resistances (as opposed to ignoring them), we can encounter the pain of having to let go of that which is no longer working for our benefit, but that we have been afraid of, or resistant, to give up.

The only way to truly know how strong our resistances are is to provoke them. Where we find ourselves clinging to a resistance, there we give birth to a dragon. Like the dragon, we must learn to confront our own resistances gently. To gently confront our resistances is to treat them with dignity and respect. We can greet them with gratitude for trying to protect us, even as we ask them to surrender themselves to new ways of coping, living and thriving. We must befriend our resistances for them to give way and allow us to walk through them. They have been guarding access to our own wounds until such time as we are ready to confront them. As creatures, who tend to follow the paths of least resistance, it can feel at first, as though we are working against our own instincts to follow our dragons into our wounds, because this is where our resistances were born. If we are doing the right work with our dragons, however, they help us walk through those resistances to greet the eternal Fire so that it can do its good work in our lives.

Even as the fire burns away what we no longer need, it also produces a renewed vitality and energy to prepare ourselves for the next adventure that awaits us. It is a journey that is ours alone to take. No one else can do it for us. These are the journeys that are meant to teach us the art of surrender, not conquest. We dare not approach the Fire with an intent to control it or put it out, for then the Fire will annihilate us. This is not a moment for willpower or pride. Those things are for other moments. When we surrender to the eternal Fire, we quickly learn that the universe opens up to us with all of its potential; that this dance between life and death is itself eternal, and that we get to experience it not once, but many times throughout our lives. To surrender oneself to the eternal Fire is to experience grace in its truest form.

We learn, in these moments, that we are connected to something much bigger than ourselves. We belong to an ecosystem of both biological and spiritual energy (which I believe are simply different manifestations of the same thing). It is in the context of these ecosystems that we learn to encounter the opposites and embrace them. We learn to both recognize and embrace that which is "me" and that which is "not me." We learn just how interdependent we are with others in our world, with the world itself and even between the disparate parts of our own individual personalities. *The Fire That Never Dies* reveals much to us when we surrender ourselves to it. It moves us beyond the tenuous syllabus of our egos to reveal our shadows and shows us that we are much more than we ever imagined. The Fire reminds us that while we may feel isolated at times, we are never completely alone. Even if we feel alone and blind to everything else around us, and within us, we are still never alone. We carry within us all the stories of our ancestors. We carry within us our own stories, both acknowledged and unacknowledged.

The art of surrender is the art of opening the door to new life. Without it, we grow stagnant and cold, miserly and stingy, suspicious and even paranoid. We can become bored, violent, or both. We stop being inquisitive and become inquisitorial. Compassion turns into nothing more than mere sentimentality. Our willpower is a tool to be employed with great wisdom and purpose, and if we have no purpose, our wills become destructive and violent because they have nothing significant or meaningful to surrender themselves to. It is our task to wake up to the purposes we have been gifted with in this life. We do not learn that purpose until we first surrender ourselves to the Fire. When we do this, we discover our true power, and we discover just how much freedom we actually have. It is the journey of the mythic hero. Joseph Campbell addresses us again, "The hero, whose attachment to ego is already annihilate, passes back and forth across the horizons of the world, in and out of the dragon, as readily as a king through all the rooms of his house."[vii]

While self-improvement is at times an admirable pursuit, the fuller context of human growth has very little to do with it. Growth has more to do with learning to accept and balance our paradoxical tensions rather than pathologizing and expending lots of energy and resources trying to overcome them. Engaging adversity is not only about exerting our willpower, it has more to do with allowing healing to transform us from within so that we make ourselves qualified and ready for the next task, the next conundrum, or even the next opportunity, to fall apart. It alerts us of our need to prepare ourselves for these moments. It requires of us an ability to identify what stories of ourselves need to die within us so that new stories and new life can spring forth. This process is not always quick and expedient, which is one of the resistances that form under the pressures of a modern, high stress, fast-paced world, that demands much of our time and attention.

We live in such a pathologically busy world, governed by the impulses of instant gratification and a dogmatic pragmatism, leaving us very little time to process anything we experience. It is no wonder the modern world is fraught with anxiety. Because we have so little time, we demand a formula, or a "quick fix," that replicates healing and then confuse that with the real thing. We want the healing without having to get our hands dirty. We want it to be expedient, so we can go about our business. Healing does not work that way. Unfortunately, our healing professions are more and more willing to accommodate this notion of a quick fix by offering simplistic and formulaic solutions for problems that may in reality be invitations to growth, rather than dilemmas to be solved. In some of our therapeutic models we are being taught to abandon our own stories and the wisdom they have to offer, rather than develop a healthy curiosity about them. Symptoms may get addressed, but the roots are never discovered or dealt with. Rather than discovering the new stories trying to emerge, we just keep repeating the old stories over and over again. A quick-fix solution, rather than inviting healing, enables us to further avoid our shadows, and hence our dragons. As our resistances strengthen, we create bigger dragons to have to deal with down the road.

There is no one formula by which we make all our pain go away, nor is there meant to be. Such a notion completely ignores and abnegates the deeply personal and unique stories we are living out each and every day. It also overlooks the importance of the pain we are experiencing. Pain can be transformed but it cannot always be eliminated completely. Our pain is a part of us just as much as our joy, and our capacity to experience both of them, makes them inextricably linked with each other. We cannot cut off different parts of ourselves because we do not like them or because they hurt. We cannot excavate ourselves from them, but we can heal our relationship with them, and healed relationships are the medicine we need to live life abundantly. It is through this healing that we teach these different parts of ourselves to let go of harmful stories about us that they have been carrying, so that they can finally experience healing and growth as well.

We also cannot control the different parts of our psyches through appeals to submission, cruelty or shame. Neither can we subvert or trick them into doing what we want through manipulation. They will not respond to those forms of cajoling and will quickly disappear from our view at the first sign that we may be getting ready to do these things. Our souls must be given space and permission to help us explore each of our inner characters, fully and without reservation. In so doing, we must be willing to listen to what each of them must say to us before we can expect them to trust us and behave as our allies.

If we are willing to risk learning how to surrender ourselves to *The Fire That Never Dies,* we may yet find ourselves capable of the re-birth and growth that a dedication to life requires. The reality of our inner lives reveals a complex mix of characters and internal dialogue between both the light and dark aspects of ourselves. If we can learn to befriend all the subtle nuances of our inner complexity, rather than resist it, then fears can become guides and resistances companions. Dragons become teachers and growth becomes a way of life rather than a single event intended to "fix" us for good and remove us permanently from the toils and complexities of life.

The word *humble* derives from the Latin word, *humus,* meaning "of the earth." When we are connected to the Earth, we are grounded. To be grounded is to be connected to *what is.* To be humble, I believe, means *to see oneself accurately.* It means that we are dedicated to reality at all costs. We consider our shortcomings, but we also acknowledge our strengths, skills and our gifts. To deny them, disregard them, or minimize them is to practice false humility. To take pride in one's own accomplishments is not the same thing as practicing arrogance, which means to practice valuing oneself over or at the expense of someone else. Arrogance teaches us that we are better, or more important than other people because of something we do well. Pride can simply be the recognition and even celebration of the things we do well. The dragons of false humility are many, and they work very hard to convince us that pride and arrogance are the same thing.

It is important that we know, to the extent that we ever can, the fullness of who we are. We need to know what we are capable of, both from the light places within us and from the dark. Not only do we learn to cherish the complexity of our own personalities by teaching ourselves to balance the various paradoxical tensions that they provoke, but to also become recipients of the creative vitality that such tensions produce. If we are unable to explore both ends of a competing tension, or the darker aspects of our nature in addition to the lighter ones, then we are missing important pieces of the whole picture.

We have lost and forgotten treasures to reclaim in those shadows. We alone are responsible for them. We also bear the responsibility to give birth to the new things trying to emerge into our mythological imagination. Our stories are invitations for all of us to learn how to allow these new gifts to be born and to cultivate them well. We will need to know and name our neglected wounds, as well as name our own unrecognized beauty and potential, both of which we learn to discover in our own shadows. If we can develop the courage to encounter all of the different parts of ourselves, along with the stories they carry with more curiosity and less shame, what needs to be transformed within us will be transformed and what needs to emerge, will emerge.

For though we are often blind to it, the truth is that we already have everything we need within us. Herein, we encounter perhaps the greatest paradoxical tension. Our journeys of growth and exploration are not about discovering what we do not yet possess but recovering and remembering what we have forgotten and what has been lost to us; the full reality of our own wholeness. We have either forgotten or not yet discovered our gifts and birthrights, and now it is time for us to have the courage to set out on a journey to retrieve them. Now is the time to heal our wounds and claim our birthrights. Now is the time to grow up.

Chapter 4
A Paradise Abandoned:
The Lambton Worm

I believe most of us would be hard-pressed to not recognize the experience of a sort of inner fragmentation, an experience that appears common to our shared human nature. Different philosophical, religious, and spiritual traditions have all contributed their own explanations for this phenomenon. Their stories and many others are all ways to account for this sense of something vital that has been lost to us as we become more aware of ourselves and have more experiences in the world. All of them attempt to help us make sense of it and bring some meaning to the grief and pain that can overcome us when we have lost something (or someone) precious to us. The great mythologist Michael Meade writes, "Each loss in life can provoke an unearthly feeling of overwhelming separation from something essential and necessary."[viii]

When we are in the midst of moments like this, it feels like our entire world has ended, and in one sense, this is true. The world, indeed, *as we have known it*, is over. When all of our plans crumble and our understanding of the world and our place in it has fallen apart, we are left with indelible scars of brokenness and inner fragmentation. To deny the painful reality of these moments is to disregard their significance. It is not through our attempts to escape the pain of moments like this that we eventually discover the gifts we stand to inherit on the other side of that pain. Pain does break us open, and in its midst, we become more open and porous to the deeper, hidden, more vulnerable parts of ourselves. In these moments, we may catch a glimpse of the much larger world our souls would have us walk into, even as we must grieve the loss of the world that has ended for us.

There is something archetypal about a deep sense of loss that initiates a quest of the soul. Often, what we must learn to also grieve the loss of is an ideal sense of Self that we have learned to cherish and protect at the expense of deeper parts of ourselves that we do not wish to see. Every time we resist, suppress, ignore or attack any knowledge about ourselves that may threaten our internal status quo, we make the inner fragmentation worse. This resistance appears from a secret desire to remain innocent, protected by the safety of what is already familiar to us, no matter how small or confining that familiarity may be. This is a wish-fulfillment on our part to remain in the relative comfort and ease of paradise, or what I like to call a "garden of innocence."

Paradise, in an unconscious state, is very womb-like, innocent, and naïve. Any notions of eternal security and safety are child-like fantasies that hearken back to this time of innocence. Part of growing up means leaving behind a good deal of certainty and security. We must acknowledge that the leaving of home (either consciously or unconsciously), or the abandonment of innocence, are both necessary and seldom accomplished without at least some trouble that disturbs the comforts of our internal status quo to get us moving into the unknown and subsequently into our own lives. A life of full consciousness and growth requires our ability to be continually thrown out of whatever comfort zones and safety nets we have grown accustomed to.

It is in these moments that we sense the precarious nature of inner work. At any time, we may choose to abandon the journey by becoming unconscious, but there is no going back into innocence. Once we become aware of something, we cannot become unaware of it. While these journeys of the soul can often prove very fulfilling, and even exciting at times, there are many opportunities to get stuck along the path if we are not paying attention, or if we turn our backs on the journeys that our souls put in front of us. This is true of us as individuals; it is also true of our communities and societies. It is true of our collective Western psyche as it finds itself lingering longer than it ought to in its own adolescence.

In order to grasp what our tasks are when we find ourselves stuck in a difficult place on our journeys, we need to understand better how we first tend to react to dangerous or frightening parts of ourselves when they reveal themselves to us. Entering into the mythological imagination to begin to understand the places where we often find ourselves stuck, I present a story called *The Curse of the Lambton Worm*. It is a wisdom story and a cautionary tale. Based on an English legend, the story of the Lambton worm provides us with our first opportunity to explore one of our Western myths about dragons and some of its assumptions about human nature, as well as the nature of good and evil itself.

The story begins with John, the privileged and somewhat licentious heir of the Lambton Castle and Estate. It is Easter Sunday, and rather than to attend church, young John has decided to go fishing, much to the chagrin and disapproving glares of the surrounding villagers, all dutifully gathering into the church. While fishing, John catches something big, but it is not a fish.

Instead, he reels in a terrible serpent on the end of his line, dripping in slime, spewing poisonous breath. When the serpent's eyes meet with John's, it chills him to the bone. Frozen by an overwhelming sense of fear and regret for his past sins and a life wasted, John sees all of this reflected in the menacing eyes of the serpent itself.

Out of both, great horror and disgust, John quickly rids himself of this vile beast by casting it into a deep, dark well. Convinced he has seen the last of this dragon, he resolves to make every effort to reform himself and become a good, faithful, and devout man. He soon leaves his village to go on a pilgrimage to the Holy Land. Little does John know that the serpent he cast in the well has not been vanquished. Rather, it has been growing large and powerful down in that old, dark well. Eventually it becomes so gigantic that it coils its enormous body around the entire hillside right next to the town which sits below, raining death and destruction down on the people of the village. The people attempt to appease its wrath by providing the dragon daily offerings of cow's milk, which seems to appease the beast long enough to offer them periodic reprieve from its menace. Every so often, a brave but foolish villager attempts to slay the dragon but always meets his demise. Efforts to cut this monster into pieces became a fool's endeavor, as the parts would simply join back together again, and the enraged serpent would strike too quickly for the attacker to launch a second campaign or even try to escape.

Eventually John, now a young man, returns from his pilgrimage to the Holy Land, only to discover to his great dismay, that this serpent he believed to have once forsaken, is wreaking havoc on all the villagers of the town. In his despair, he consults a nearby witch for advice on how to slay the dragon once and for all. She provides him with a special armor adorned with large spikes that, when used, will prevent the dragon's body from reforming. John succeeds, but the caveat to finally doing away with the dragon's curse is that he must also slay the first living thing he sees after defeating the dragon. Much to John's despair, it is his father who is first to greet him. John cannot bring himself to kill his father, so he opts to kill his most prized dog instead, hoping that this substitute will pass as a satisfactory sacrifice. It does not, and for nine generations after John's fateful mistake, all the heirs of Lambton Castle would meet horrible ends.

Young John represents the restlessness of youth and the impulse to rebel from that which has been prescribed for him as a good, pious, and righteous life, and to begin to discover what is valuable about life on his own terms. This process of rebellion, while irritating for parents of teenagers, is nevertheless an important developmental stage and rite of passage that all our youth must pass through. If we had no opportunities to become restless and disgruntled with the status quo of youth, we would never leave the comfortable womb of our parent's homes, traditions, beliefs, and ideas, and learn to become responsible adults. Growth, or the process of individuation, requires multiple moments of crises for us to face in our lives, otherwise we would have no reason to grow, learn, and develop our own values. We would have no reason to leave the nest!

John is looking for an excuse to rebel, which is to say, he is looking for an opportunity to practice his first steps toward individuation, autonomy, and adulthood. He soon learns that, while this opportunity to rebel is important and necessary, it comes at a price. It is interesting that the story has John choosing Easter Sunday as his moment to do this. To emphasize the point of the *sacred* (often, another word for the status quo) he is choosing to rebel against it by going fishing. It is important to note here, that many of our Western myths are rooted in an assumed conflict between God and nature, particularly as the Christian tradition worked hard to define itself over and against the early Pagan traditions. John's choice to go fishing, rather than join the Easter worship is symbolic of the 'sin' of choosing nature over God, and hence a profound rejection of those moral principles which undergird the good, church-going folk of the town.

Going fishing, here, is a metaphor for John's unconscious impulse to begin exploring his own wisdom apart from the prescribed wisdom of his community. This urge is so powerful, that, to come to terms with how important this task is, it must be framed as a conflict between that which appears as sacred and that which appears profane to get John's attention to the inner longing of his soul to discover who he is on his own terms.

It should be noted, that while John is responding to a stirring in his soul, he is still very unconscious. He has little understanding of the impulses driving his behavior. He is not working to understand the inner depths of his soul. He would just rather go fishing than go to church. Few of us have any idea what stirs in the depths of our souls, particularly when cast in the throes of youthful innocence. Nevertheless, the human shadow is reaching out to tell us something about ourselves, even though our own ignorance and naiveté. The serpent he reels in on his fishing line, symbolizes his first encounter with his own shadow, and predictably, he is horrified by it.

He has no idea what he is going to find in the river when he first sets out to go fishing. His innocence and naiveté actually serve him well here, for if he had any inkling of what he was about to discover in the river, he would never have gone fishing in the first place. The same is true of most of us when we "go fishing," meaning our first adventurous journeys into the unknown. If we had any sense what we might encounter, we would never make the journey in the first place. We often begin these journeys with a kind of naïve hope and optimism that gets us out the door of our own comfort zones. In this way, our innocence serves us well, at least initially.

Unwittingly, John hooks the dragon that has long lived in the depths of his soul, his soul here symbolized by the water of the river. Water is often a universal symbol for soul in many spiritual and mythological traditions. This first encounter with his own shadow is far too much for him, however. In a flash, he encounters the knowledge of both good and evil within himself. He becomes aware of his own missed opportunities, a sense of his own shame, and the capacity for his own darkness. He does not like what he sees and makes quick work to get rid of this vile beast in hopes of never having to encounter it again.

John does what many of us do when we encounter such a moment; scramble furiously to "do the right thing," to makes amends with ourselves and flee from the terror now staring us in the eyes, to avoid having to feel the pain of facing our own shadows. In this case, John embraces religion via his pilgrimage to the Holy Land, for his *mea culpa*. The journey into the Holy Land serves as a metaphor for what I call a flight into the light, where salvation becomes more a mechanism of avoidance than thoughtful reflection and transformation. It makes sense that John would seek to correct his sin by making a pilgrimage to the Holy Land, since John has committed a profane act by choosing to go fishing rather than going to church, which resulted in his awareness of the dragon. John senses some kind of divine retribution at work to which he now must make amends for, and quickly. John believes that this is the action he must take to make everything all right again, and hopefully avoid ever having to encounter anything so terrifying within himself ever again.

The problem is, when we take these sudden steps to make amends for ourselves, we are not setting out to engage in transformative growth, at least not initially. We are unconsciously looking to escape or avoid our shadows in the hope that they will just go away if we do enough of the right things over and over again to erase our dark potential and makes amends for its existence. John sets out, as many of us do when we acknowledge some dark principle alive in us, to make his life right, and learn to do the right things. In and of itself, this seems like the good thing to do, and John certainly does mature, gaining wisdom from his journey. One may reasonably assume that John has learned something of value during his pilgrimage to the Holy Land.

The problem is that he has yet to face his dragon, not understanding that this dragon belongs to him, mistakenly believing it to be gone forever. In leaving behind what he believes to be the monster he will never have to encounter again; he also abandons his home and all of the people that live within it. We can recognize, in this example, "home" as a metaphor for wholeness. John, upon meeting his shadow, becomes aware for the first time in his life, his own feelings of inner fragmentation. This instigates a journey for him to go retrieve what has been lost. The leaving of home was the initial loss of innocence, but John has been frightened back into a state of unconsciousness. His first encounter with his shadow was not pleasant. He is happy to leave it behind and make that the end of the story. However, again, while he may have retreated into a state of unconsciousness, he cannot go back into innocence. Sooner or later, the dragon comes back, and usually the dragon has become bigger, stronger, and far more menacing.

For John, of course, his time spent learning in the Holy Land is not the end of the story. The village represents the rest of the other abandoned parts of his own psyche, left behind in his desperate attempt to flee his own shadow. In denying his human dark potential, he has unwittingly abandoned other unconscious elements of his soul, now relegated as well to his shadow. As such, the rest of the town has been left to the mercy of a dragon, growing fat and powerful in the brooding dark, until it becomes so big that it engulfs an entire hillside above the village. The size of the dragon grows in proportion to the amount of time that the dragon has been ignored or suppressed. This is an important psychological principle, if not an important spiritual principle as well. The villagers do everything they can to appease the beast, and a few brave souls even attempt to slay the dragon, which is a death sentence for all of them. The dragon does not allow his attackers a second chance to slay it or flee from it. Interestingly enough, neither the fight nor flight impulse can save them from their doom.

At this point in the story, we can infer that John must have had some awareness, however unconsciously, that it was important for him to return to the home of his youth. Some insight has broken into his awareness that he left some pretty important parts of himself behind that now need to be retrieved and taken care of. He does not yet have enough awareness to predict what he will find when he returns, however, and is completely caught off guard and horrified to discover that the dragon is not only alive and well, but has multiplied in size and wrath. Laying waste to his tiny village. John now encounters his shadow for the second time. Again, he must face the terror he once abandoned when he was much younger, only this time the terror has grown much larger and more menacing. This dragon will no longer be ignored.

John is now aware that he cannot escape his shadow, but instead of facing it he goes looking for someone he can bargain with that might provide him with a way out of having to face his dragon. He is appealing to the magical principle here, looking for a quick and binding solution for his troubles. Fear is still the primary motivating factor for John's subsequent actions. This is often when we go looking to a priest, a guru or even a therapist for help, perhaps hoping to find some bargain they can help us make with our own dragons to go away and leave us alone. It is this fear, however, that can also provide us with the initial impulse and energy we need to prepare ourselves to face our own dragons. If we are working with a good clergy person or a good therapist, they will teach us how to repurpose our quest for healing from one of aggression or avoidance to our dragons, to one of curiosity and inner reconciliation with them.

There are more steps to take once this awareness has been activated. It is here that we must pay careful attention, because our next steps are very important in determining which direction we will go. The next steps of this drama for John begin with a wish-fulfillment fantasy that he can magically bargain his way out of facing his dragon properly. The witch in this story represents the magical principle that John is looking for. John bargains with the witch in exchange for a final solution to rid himself of his dragon. The witch is clever though and understands the principle that there is always a price to pay for such actions. She can provide the trick he needs, but there is a catch. If he is going to be willing to murder his dragon, he must be willing to murder another person (psychologically speaking, another part of himself). In fact, it must be the "first living thing" he sees after the dragon is dead, which unfortunately turns out to be his father.

There are at least two ways to interpret the significance of the father showing up at this point in the story. The psychological task here is to either integrate the father principle, meaning John must accept the task of awakening himself to his inner father-function, and take responsibility for it, or to wean himself from the outward father figure, whose approval he awaits before making his own decisions and accepting responsibility for them. Either one requires John to "kill" his father to accomplish the task. John is not yet conscious enough to understand this dilemma however, and his next choice, unfortunately, brings disaster.

John does not choose to let go of his need for an outward father, who can tell him what to do, so that he can be relieved of that responsibility for himself. Instead John chooses to try to outwit this dilemma by circumventing it altogether and choosing a living being that he tries to convince himself is sacred to him, but is actually disposable, which is his prize dog. In this sense, John becomes his own trickster in order to avoid having to face the consequences of his actions when he strikes his bargain with the witch.

We are all quite accustomed to playing these kinds of little psychological tricks on ourselves. John's choice to kill his prize dog serves as little more than an evasion and a distraction from what he must actually face and take responsibility for, which is the dragon he gave birth to.

John has found a clever new way to avoid his shadow and the discomfort it brings. He chooses not to heed the instructions of the witch, and as a result, the heirs of his kingdom suffer for nine generations. Nine generations are a long time. John was meant to be a king. Instead, he settled for saving face and avoiding the responsibility necessary to become a king. How often do we choose to reject our own inner gold and royalty in favor of an easier path? How many little lies do we tell ourselves on a daily basis to appease our fears and bargain with our insecurities in order to avoid taking responsibility for them? One can hardly blame John for his impulses, and yet his inability to take responsibility for himself only leads to disaster for him.

The story of a continued failure to make peace with our dragons and come to terms with the shadows from whence they come is our story. Living in a light-centric society where we avoid the shadowy aspects of life at all costs, encourages us to make these bargains with the magical principle to avoid having to face the things we do not want to face, lying as they do, in the dark. Salvation, when we deny or ignore our own shadows, ceases to be a quest that we ourselves are responsible for, hoping that someone else can do our work for us. We would rather it be something bestowed upon us or something we can purchase. Light then ceases to be a symbol of truth and becomes instead, a tool we ironically use to hide from our own shadows. The more forcefully we attempt to strengthen the principles of the light at the expense of those of the dark, the larger the split we create inside of ourselves and the further we are from our own healing and wholeness.

We are responsible for the devil within, not the other way around, and the devil only grows as powerful and dangerous as our refusal to acknowledge and engage it within us. Instead, we build up a façade of strength, predicated on the belief that we are "in the light" while others are "in the dark;" that we are "right" and that those who oppose us are "wrong." When we use those two words, we automatically establish a dualism, which will often sabotage the possibility of a reconciliation with our shadows, as it does in our relationships with other people. We also fail to acknowledge the existence of our shadows, because we have made the bargain and performed the magic trick that we think will appease our conscience enough to forget that we left an unattended dragon brooding and growing large and vengeful from our neglect, in the dark.

The paradise of the womb of innocence cannot hold us in its bliss forever. We are either consciously or unconsciously predisposed to abandon this paradise, for we cannot become conscious and rediscover our wholeness any other way. If we do not go looking for trouble ourselves, trouble will come to find us eventually. The paradise of the womb must ultimately be disrupted and abandoned over and over again. We will experience the pain of losing our innocence, but as we grow up, we learn that these kinds of losses are important and necessary for our growth.

Through this story, we become aware of our own sense of inner fragmentation; that loss of something essential to us that looms over the loneliness of the Western soul. We also see how we automatically reject, often multiple times and in multiple ways, the very parts of ourselves that provide the clues we need to rediscover that original wholeness we had forgotten, which is what can bring us the healing and peace we are looking for.

Once our dragons make themselves known to us, we can no longer pretend they do not exist. We are now responsible for them whether we like it or not. We may choose to fall back into unconsciousness, but the fact that innocence is forever lost ensures that we will meet the dragon over and over again until we agree to finally face it and surrender to the task of taming it and receiving its power and wisdom. With each step that we take further into our own lives, we leave innocence behind and walk into greater awareness and wholeness.

We are meant to leave the initial womb of paradise, for we do not gain the wisdom, strength, courage, and awareness required of us to re-discover our wholeness by staying there. It is inevitable that paradise must be fundamentally lost before it can be found again with conscious awareness. Whenever we feel cast out of our own paradises of innocence, we are given the opportunity to take an important journey, which is the journey of the soul.

We do not know what happens to John and his heirs after their long nine-generation exodus in the wilderness. Psychologically speaking, we know that the story never ends for us. John will have another chance to face his dragon and come to terms with it, just as we are given countless opportunities to do the same. That is the hope that we always have available to us, no matter how accustomed we have become at bargaining away our lives in exchange for a false sense of safety and security, which never really comes. Eventually, we must allow ourselves to be thrown out of all our nests and get moving along down the road.

Chapter 5
Ouroboros: The Dragon That Eats Itself

Garet Garrett writes of the condition of the Western soul; "One story of us is continuous. It is the story of our struggle to recapture the Garden of Eden, meaning by that a state of existence free from the doom of toil."[ix] The second creation story in Genesis, Chapter Two of the Hebrew Bible presents a myth by which we derive one of our origin stories in the West. Psychologically speaking, it represents this tension between innocence and awareness and the drama that ensues when we move from one to the other. As has been established, once awareness is attained, one cannot return to innocence. Once Adam and Eve attained the knowledge of good and evil, they could no longer remain in their garden of innocence. Such is the story of us when we become conscious and pursue our paths of growth and inner reconciliation.

Innocence and awareness are archetypal themes. The tension that exists between the two of them can provide us with the energy we need to exercise our ability to increase self-awareness. We have no choice, once innocence has been lost, but to move forward and grow up. For with each piece of knowledge we acquire, we become responsible for it whether we like it or not. It is at this crossroads between innocence and awareness, as we learned in the previous chapter, that we often discover dragons. We can often feel tempted by the desire to fall back into the blissful innocence of the womb, but that is no longer possible, even though we all consciously or unconsciously look for opportunities to find a way back.

The harder we fight to try and regain entrance back into the garden of innocence, the more fragmented we become, and the further we are from peace. Growth is forward, not backward. We cannot unlearn what we have learned. Awareness expands rather than contracts. We are creatures who are meant to learn how to love, and that process begins by first learning how to love ourselves in full awareness and full acceptance of who we are, as we are. We cannot love ourselves or others fully in the naiveté of innocence. Real love requires deeper levels of awareness and a commitment to the reality of the complex nature of ourselves and of our meaningful relationships.

With awareness comes the awakening of the drama between life and death. This is a drama that is playing out all the time. Even if we try to deny death, that still does not stop it from happening, whether it is the final death of our mortal coil, or the many smaller, but no less important psychological deaths we must endure throughout the courses of our lives. Failure to accept death as an integral part of life means a failure to fully live and ensures that we will get ourselves stuck somewhere. The reality of this tension between life and death is a looming paradox that encompasses all of us, and we are meant to learn how to balance the uncomfortable tension between both as a necessary part of what it means to grow up and become whole human beings.

This paradoxical tension of life and death is symbolized by the *Ouroboros*, which is the depiction of a dragon or serpent eating its own tail. The Ouroboros is an ancient symbol. It is a powerful symbol in the world of alchemy, as well as depth psychology. It can represent many things. One way to interpret the Ouroboros is of a greedy dragon so consumed by its own gluttony and avarice that it begins to eat itself once it has devoured everything else around it, having nothing else to devour. Since it only knows how to consume, it must consume itself after consuming everything else. In this sense, the dragon is completely unconscious and possessed by its own appetites. It has no awareness that it is eating itself to death. It is only governed by its appetite and pathological need to consume. In remains unconscious, and acts out of a wholly destructive, thoughtless, and greedy instinctual drive.

Another way of interpreting this symbol is that the dragon is fully aware of what it is doing. It chooses to consume itself because it knows that its death is necessary for life itself to continue, and new life to spring forth. Instead of consuming out of mere greed or blind instinct, it is exercising the wisdom of self-sacrifice for the greater good. In this sense, it mimics the journey of the Phoenix.

Here we have two different interpretations of the Ouroboros. It may be tempting for us to choose one over the other because we find one more appealing, and because we also desire to rescue ourselves from the tension between the two. The Ouroboros, however, reminds us that its very nature is to inhabit the worlds of duality. It is both selfish and selfless. It is both conscious and unconscious. It is both blind and aware at the same time. It both consumes and is consumed. The Ouroboros is *us*. This dance between innocence and awareness, self-indulgence and self-sacrifice, is a central theme to the particular conundrums of many of the mythologies of the Western world as well.

An Ouroboros then, is a primordial symbol for the balancing of opposites. When we wrestle with these particular paradoxes, we must learn how to rely on more than our normal judgment, which is a function we have cultivated to navigate our lives in the outside world. The rules can change quickly, however, when it comes to interpreting symbols, creatures and characters that our unconscious minds produce, and often show up in our dreams. Our soul has its own wisdom that is not dependent upon the rules with which have developed to navigate our waking lives. Our soul sends images our way which our egos have a difficult time making sense of for reasons that will be covered in a later chapter. It is one of our tasks in life to learn how to admit these strange images into our awareness and learn how to sit with them and eventually work with them.

In Robert A. Johnson's book, *Balancing Heaven and Earth*[x], he describes an encounter with a giant snake in one of his dreams. In the dream, he is being pursued by the snake, which is a type of dragon. He recalls running as fast as he can from this giant menace, but no matter how fast he runs, the snake keeps pace with him. Eventually, he notices the head and neck of the snake overtaking him, looming over his head as he continues to run. Johnson would later discover, through his process of dream interpretation, that the snake, far from trying to harm him, was attempting to guide and protect him. Johnson identified the presence of the large snake as a symbol that signified great change about to occur in his life. The snake, with its ability to shed its own skin periodically to emerge into a new skin, serves as a powerful symbol for the great transitions between death and re-birth.

I had a snake dream of my own in early adulthood. This dream occurred before I made the decision to go to graduate school to become a therapist. In the dream, I was in a cabin in the mountains with a small group of friends. The mood was light, and everyone was having a good time when everything suddenly became very quiet and tense in the room. We all had the immediate awareness of a giant snake sitting right outside the door of the cabin, waiting to get inside and devour all of us. There was some discussion as to what we should do, and how we should remove the threat of the snake.

The consensus was that I was to be the one to kill it. I grabbed a nearby baseball bat and approached the door cautiously. I knew I would have to be very quick, quicker than the snake, if I was to survive. My friends all gathered behind me as I went to open the door. As I began to level the bat toward the snake's head, everything seemed to descend into slow motion. The snake had raised its head up to the level of my face but was not attempting to strike. I remember watching the look on the snake's face as the bat was in motion. The expression on its face was of pure terror, which then turned into utter rage as my bat met its skull and dropped the snake dead on the porch. Everyone behind me cheered and breathed a sigh of relief. I, however, was left with the nauseating feeling that I had made a terrible mistake. I remember weeping when I woke up in the morning. I did not feel strong or courageous. I felt weak and ashamed. For the next two days, I was a mess.

The snake in my dream was a prophetic manifestation of great change about to befall my life. I was so resistant to it at the time that I killed the snake in my dream. I have been working hard to honor the presence and the memory of that snake ever since. My failure with the snake is representative of a fear that goes well beyond the inner workings of my own psyche. It is a collective fear we all share, which is the fear of change, and ultimately a manifestation of the fear of death. Change might mean that we must lose or let go of some things we have acquired or grown accustomed to. If we are constantly in fear of being robbed, hoodwinked or taken advantage of, then we will hold on even tighter. We will never let go. If, however, we learn the art of surrender, we may stand a chance to learn something important about the paths we must follow. We cannot escape the pain of loss, or the grief we experience when the time to let go of that which no longer belongs to us comes. The grieving process, however, helps us to clear away the space to make room for something new to emerge.

Whether we run from the threat, as Johnson was attempting to do in his dream, or we fight it, as I did in my dream, we lose. We lose the wisdom, the lesson, and the vitality needed from these serpents to usher us into the next stages or phases of our lives, increasing our wisdom and abundance. In effect, we stunt our own growth. It is because we have never been taught to tame dragons that we find ourselves stuck in the same conflicts over and over again.

Once we discover a dragon; one that we have created, one that has been imposed upon us, or an archetypal dragon that has been lying in wait for us in the collective unconscious; we have no idea how to react to it. We have not been equipped because we no longer have meaningful rituals in our culture designed to christen us with our birthrights and equip us to greet death. Our birthrights are the necessary gifts that must be awakened in us by a community that prepares us for the passages we must take when we move out of childhood into adolescence and from adolescence into adulthood. These rituals, if they are done properly, are designed to concretize our birthrights, so that we are prepared to share the gifts they bring with the world around us. They are also meant to teach us how to face and tame our dragons. In the absence of these meaningful rituals, we are not prepared, and we will choose the fight or flight response every time, because no one has given us a third option to even consider, much less practice.

Whenever our fears become intolerable to us, we project them onto others, and this is where hatred is born. Hate is a powerful dragon. It is what will manifest from our failure to tame it. Internally we will project our rage onto the dragon itself and commit an act of internal violence against ourselves. Outwardly we will commit violence upon others. This rage is what mirrored the face of the snake I confronted right before I murdered it in my dream. It was a warning, but also an invitation to make the changes I ultimately needed to make to accept my own destiny. In accepting responsibility for that destiny, I also had to come to terms with my own capacity to destroy, an insight that I initially did not want to acknowledge or accept but needed to if I was going to become a responsible adult and a responsible therapist. If I cannot come to terms with my ability to hurt others, then I will hurt them unconsciously. Awareness is vital for our ability to cultivate compassion and restraint where it is necessary.

Perhaps one of the reasons why our dragons appear so threatening and evil to us is because we have given them no other choice but to carry all our darkness for us instead of taking responsibility for it ourselves. Instead of learning to face and take responsibility for our own shadows, we have instead built an economy of projecting those shadows onto others. The maxim *might makes right* is very much at the forefront of our current codex of our pragmatic, Western values. Rather than having to admit that we might be wrong (which we experience as defeat or showing weakness), we would rather deny there is a problem altogether (flight), or wage war with anyone who might question whether there is a problem to begin with (fight). That we recognize these traits so powerfully in the various leaders of our political and financial institutions is not surprising but should be much more troubling to us than most of us are capable of acknowledging. Sadly, we continue to confuse the fight response with strength, and our world is suffering greatly as a result. Rather than resisting the urges of dictatorial forms of leadership, we hail and worship them as models of strength and resolve.

It has not occurred to us yet, that true power has nothing to do with conquest. True power involves a fierce love and an ability to both, stand up for oneself and defend others, as well as a willingness to engage in personal sacrifice when needed. True power understands the importance of balancing this paradoxical tension. True power also manifests in an ability to cultivate love and empathy. There is no other quest more difficult, messy or praiseworthy than to put oneself in the vulnerable position of bearing witness to someone else's experience, particularly their pain. True power invites us to remain grounded in each and every moment without escaping too far into the past or the future. In this sense, to be caught in an unguarded moment can become an experience we can learn to greet with joy and curiosity, rather than fear or shame.

We have been taught that vulnerability is weakness. We have been encouraged to always be on our guard, never show our cards, and never risk being made a fool of. The problem is that we never learn the wisdom of the fool! As we pour all our energy into avoiding these pitfalls, we also avoid living our lives. We cannot truly know who we are if we are constantly feeling the need to defend and protect ourselves. We cannot truly know who we are until we are allowed to make our own mistakes, become aware our own weaknesses as well as our strengths, and come to terms with our own fragility and vulnerability alongside our own inner wisdom and strengths.

We have so much to offer by simply being who we are, and part of who we are, are creatures meant for journeys into deeper levels of awareness, joy, compassion, and fidelity to our own healing and wholeness. The joy that is our birthright to receive and experience, is embedded in our ability to keep moving and learn as much as we can about ourselves and the world around us. Our happiness is not in the destination of any one "rose," but in the journey itself. There are always more roses for us to discover. Occasionally we find a rose that we really fall for, and are tempted to settle down with, but we cannot linger forever. We do not get to keep the rose. We must be able to grieve the loss of it when it is time to let it go and clear the necessary space to accept the new rose presented to us with its own fresh and unique wisdom.

As creatures of curiosity, we are driven to both experience and understand our world. When we can fulfill this task with generosity, we learn what we need to learn when we need to learn it. Curiosity must be taught and cultivated like any other virtue. Curiosity is what allows us to make mistakes and experience failure without having to burden ourselves with undue judgment and shame. Curiosity is what allows us to learn something important from these experiences.

The myth of the Ouroboros teaches us that life and death are bound together in an endless cycle. It does bring death and destruction, but it also brings the promise of new life. It teaches us just how important it is for us to work every day at becoming more aware of every part of ourselves, so that we do not remain unconscious. It teaches us that if we become stuck for too long, we are likely to become lost and hardened beyond the capacity to grow any further. We may even forget what it is that we have lost, even as we wander endlessly and aimlessly to retrieve something that we feel is missing, not knowing what it is. This feeling of being eternally, unconsciously lost has become our inheritance as modern, Western people. It is the feeling of "half-ness," or inner fragmentation that we carry. Perhaps we can attempt to understand the source of this half-ness on our way toward reengaging with wholeness again. After all, it does us no good to look for the half that is missing if we do not even know what the other half is, or even worse; if we are unaware that we are even have a missing half in the first place.

Chapter 6
Syzygy and the Half-Man:
The Divine Feminine and
Masculine Split

The word *divine*, I believe, can be used interchangeably with the words "eternal," or "archetypal," at least where the purpose of myth is concerned. It symbolizes a timeless, enduring force that moves through all living things, giving them breath and being. When speaking about the Divine Feminine or Divine Masculine, it is important that these terms are not to be confused with sex or gender. They are divine energies that we all share as human beings, regardless of gender or sexual orientation, and every human being is called to actualize both energies within themselves. They are powerful and integral components of our own wholeness. As such, when we only choose to identify with one side of the divine wholeness and neglect or abandon the other side, we create trouble for ourselves and trouble for the world around us.

It is in this particular conflict between the Divine Feminine and Divine Masculine energies, that so many of our Western dragons are born. It is in the denial of, or outright hostility toward, either the feminine or masculine aspects of our souls that much suffering is, has been, and continues to exert its toll. At the moment, the Western world is suffering from a Patriarchal dominance that favors an unbalanced and toxic form of masculinity at the almost total expense of the feminine. The dragons that spring from the Western world's ethic of patriarchal dominance over nature (as an entity to be conquered rather than nurtured) represent a dangerous and unconscious form of both inner and outer fragmentation, divorced as it is, from the Divine Feminine. This split is centuries old. As such it is not easily challenged or healed. Men, in many ways, have been benefitting from this split in enough ways that the privilege that comes along with it is not easily relinquished.[1] Because it is so old and so ingrained, it makes our task to restore this divine split to its original wholeness much more urgent. It not only threatens the well-being of our souls; it threatens the well-being of the planet we live on. Our failure to incorporate the Divine Feminine back into our collective imaginations will have grave consequences for the future of our planet and our species.

The following story a well-known fairy tale that conveys the truths and consequences of such a split between the Divine Feminine and Masculine and gives us some insight into our predicament as people living with the phenomenon of such a grand divorce. It is the tale of *Briar Rose*, or Sleeping Beauty, as she is more commonly known to us. The tale of Briar Rose is a story that, like so many other stories, has been misunderstood and misinterpreted in a world that has forgotten the language of myth, as well as a world that has discarded and suppressed the enduring power of the Divine Feminine. Many of us are familiar with Disney's rendition of the story, in which Sleeping Beauty must be saved (and thereby legitimized) by the true love's kiss of a handsome prince. This is an interpretation of the story told through the lenses of our patriarchal paradigm. Indeed, this is the only interpretation of the story that the patriarchal paradigm is capable of producing. What if, however, we were to step outside of that paradigm for a moment? What might we see that is different?

In the original story of Briar Rose, it is not just she who has fallen into a deep stupor. The whole kingdom has fallen asleep (unconscious) along with her. The circumstances are dire, for the kingdom is not safe in such an unprotected state. Briar Rose represents the rejected Divine Feminine archetype. The handsome prince represents the Divine Masculine archetype that has done the rejecting. The handsome prince once believed that he was just fine on his own, and that he had everything under control, all by himself. Not so. At some point, he must have realized that he was missing something essential. At some point, this need to reconnect with what was lost drove him on a quest to find Briar Rose and reawaken her.

As it happens, Briar Rose is not the one that needs saving after all. Rather, it is the handsome prince along with the rest of the kingdom that needs saving. They have been suffering from her absence because the Divine Feminine has

---

[1] I believe that men have also been, and continue to be, victims of this patriarchal dominance in the sense that they have been unable to develop some of the more relational wisdom and faculties traditionally reserved for females, robbing them of a necessary wisdom and wholeness which we must all develop, again regardless of sex or gender.

been suppressed (put to sleep). It has not been allowed to actively contribute toward the health and well-being of the kingdom, as it was designed to, and so the kingdom is dying. Briar Rose's strength and wisdom are the keys to the restoration of the kingdom and its ability to be whole and strong once again. It is vital that she be awakened at once to rescue the kingdom from its stupor, so that everyone in it will become conscious again.

The prince understands that he belongs to Briar Rose and she to him in a divine union; the union of the Divine Feminine and the Divine Masculine. This is not a union of dominance and submission. It is a union of equally powerful forces designed to nurture and inform each other with equal purpose and care. Fate or destiny (or both) intervened at some point to help the prince awaken to this realization and rediscover what he had originally rejected, but desperately needed. The story has a happy ending, of course, because the handsome prince eventually comes to his senses and seeks to join again, with the Divine Feminine. Our current capacity to recognize this conundrum in the West, however, is much more troubling. Unlike the handsome prince, there is a great denial and suppression of awareness that something has gone missing. There is no acknowledgment that there is a vital quest to recapture something that has been long since rejected and lost to us. I have chosen to create my own little parable below to illustrate the conundrum I believe we currently find ourselves in.

Syzygy and the Half-Man

The term Syzygy comes from the ancient Greek word *suzugos,* which means "yoked together." It represents a pair of opposites that belong to each other in a union. Carl Jung used the term to refer to these dichotomous principles that he identified in men as the *anima,* or Divine Feminine energy, and *animus* in women, the Divine Masculine energy. Syzygy embodies the pairing of opposites to signify that the nature of life, in its purest essence, is union. As an exercise for us to again enter the mythic imagination, I offer this small tale called *Syzygy and the Half-Man* as an invitation for us to explore the context of this crisis in the modern West.

At the beginning of time, whereby manifest became the divine principles of the unity between masculine and feminine, the Syzygy was born. At some point along the way, the half of Syzygy, that was the masculine part, began to wonder what it would be like to experience the world on his own, and so he tore himself away from Syzygy. When he did this, he became a Half-Man. He appears as a Half-Man, because he is only half of a divine union. He proclaimed himself as emancipated from the divine unity, and so claimed his own identity and confused his half-ness with wholeness. He reveled in his own "is-ness" but the price he paid for it was that he was now destined to walk around in a half-way, speak in a half-way, think about things in a half-way, and see the world in a half-way. When he tells the story of his birth, he can only tell half of the story. He only remembers his birth as his emancipation from the Divine Feminine half. He is meant to be re-joined with her, but he has long-forgotten that she exists, and so continues to pursue his own exploits in a world of his own making, a half-world.

Feeling unencumbered, he wanders the Earth, convincing others to join him in his half-ness, for despite his new-found sense of autonomy, he still longs for connection with others. He appears to others as untethered in some way, master of his own fate, and so many find themselves attracted by his invitation to come join him and live in their own half-ness just as he does. He is very charismatic in his fervor to establish a half-world populated with half-people. Many others begin to claim their half-ness with him, and his half-world begins to grow.

Because he has rejected wholeness, he looks to create his own version of it in his half-ness as he builds the half-world, not able to see that he creates this half-world in his own half-image. There is no acknowledgment that anything might be missing in the half-world of the Half-Man. If anyone should dare suggest this, it serves to provoke his ire, and that is intolerable to him. There is no need for wisdom in the Half-Man's half-world, because wisdom is the practice of making room for what one does not yet know and what one has not yet learned. Certainty, not wisdom, is the guiding principle of the half-world. In the Half-Man's half-world, he believes that he sees everything that there is to see and knows everything that there is to know. In the Half-Man's half-world, keeping the peace means "keeping things the way that they have always been." In the Half-Man's half-world, the purpose of an education is to learn to maximize one's utility, not increase one's wisdom. The half-world of the Half-Man does not expand but remains static. His half-world is like a steady clock that must always run smoothly in the same way for all of time

If there is a problem anywhere in the good functioning of the clock-like nature of his half-world, the defective part(s) must be identified, removed and replaced. This is how problems are handled in the half-world of the Half-Man. There is no need for diagnosis, care or cure. The defective parts are simply removed and replaced. There is nothing further to understand about them, except that they no longer function, and have lost their usefulness. In this way, he sees only half of the problem, but believes himself to see the whole problem. Naturally he is only able to attend to the half of the problem that he sees, while the other half goes unnoticed and neglected. If someone tries to convince him that there exists something from the other half of the world that he cannot see, he becomes very agitated and even vengeful. Such a vulgar suggestion threatens to derail the good and steady functioning of his clock-like half-world.

There are no artists or prophets in the half-world of the Half-Man. Such people are a disturbance and a distraction. At best, they are amusing entertainment, but nothing more. If they start to become too disruptive, the Half-Man must intervene. Such people must be silenced or removed, by force if necessary, to keep the Half-Man's half-world from falling into disarray. Order and piety are among some of the more important virtues of the half-world.

Because he is a Half-Man, he can only speak and understand the language of the half-world. If anybody from the other half tries to speak to him, he cannot comprehend what they are saying. If they continue talking to him, then he begins to grow very agitated. He tells the other half that it should not speak, and that it should be put in its place, and that it needs to begin to obey the rules established in the half-world, governed only by those few the Half-Man has chosen to govern for the good functioning of the half-world. If one cannot obey the rules, then they must be punished until they are made to only acknowledge the half-reality of the Half-Man's half-world.

Eventually the Half-Man's half-world, of which he has spent much toil building, perfecting and maintaining, becomes the only world that the Half-Man has ever known, as he has quite forgotten all about the divine unity from whence, he came. If he himself grows sick, he can only find the remedy he needs from the half that he has rejected, but because the Half-Man has forgotten about the original unity, he wanders around his half-world only with the vague sense that something is missing, that he is only a half. He has trained himself to reject this feeling, as he has trained himself to reject many feelings, as an unfortunate, leftover by-product of an irrationality that he deplores and works very hard to conquer and rid himself of by his sheer will. Because he has lost all knowledge of the original unity that he came from, he walks in despair, not knowing that he is only a half, not understanding that he needs the other half, continuously looking from within his own half-ness for the remedy he vaguely surmises he needs but cannot find in order to feel whole again.

I believe that the initial split that occurs at the beginning of this story could symbolize a kind of necessary de-coupling in order to make conscious awareness possible. In order for innocence to yield to consciousness, in other words, a separation from the original unity has to take place. If the syzygy is going to gain the capacity to reflect on itself with any kind of objectivity, it needs to be able to observe itself. Here, the masculine principle, shared and exercised by all people, becomes responsible for this task by first becoming aware of its own separateness. If, however, union with awareness is the final purpose of this quest, as I believe it is, then it ought to be assumed that the masculine half of the syzygy is meant to be reunited with its divine counterpart.

The plight of the Half-Man symbolizes the reification of a divided soul as an end unto itself as opposed to a path toward the deeper awareness of a need to rediscover the divine union with consciousness. This is the conclusion the handsome prince must come to in order to instigate his journey back to Briar Rose. The Half-Man's willful ignorance and re-structuring of this story line, however, is undergirded by centuries of patriarchal dominance in the Western world.

When we live out of our own half-ness, the world presents itself as a system of dualities of endless conflict with no opportunity for reconciliation. The inclination is that human nature is not to be embraced, but rather fought, suppressed or transcended. Human nature becomes then, an impediment to perfection, and must be conquered by the will, or by a Supreme Being that can cleanse it of the sins of imperfection. When the Half-Man encounters a dragon, he only knows how to slay the dragon. The dragon appears to him only as an evil that threatens the status quo of his half-ness and that half-kingdom he has built. Joseph Campbell writes, "The removal of the feminine into another form symbolizes the beginning of the fall from perfection into duality; 'humankind' is cut off from not only the vision but even the recollection of the image of God."[xi]

Cut off from the original source of life, the Half-Man's counterpart in the Divine Feminine, he wanders around believing he is entirely a product of his own will and his own creation. He represents the apex of the ethical imperatives of rugged individualism. He expects others to adopt his belief in his own half-world, and if they do not, they are punished severely, as this is an indictment of him. He cannot tolerate a different interpretation of life. In his world, there is only ever a clear right answer and a wrong answer in any given moment for any given situation. No ambiguity or complexity is permitted. In fact, ambiguity and complexity are interpreted by him as a weakness, a distraction or an outright threat to his power. Truth, he proclaims, does not require our investigation or curiosity, for it should be immediately obvious to anyone and everyone. In his world, there is no need for discernment or critical thinking.

As stated earlier, patriarchy is a failure to see that all people, regardless of gender or sexual orientation, carry both feminine and masculine aspects of their nature within them, and that every human being on the journey toward wholeness must be free to accept and exercise both energies freely and appropriately. The concept of will and surrender are two sides of the same coin if they are consciously working together as a unity. Under patriarchal dominance, however, these virtues have been at endless war with each other. Patriarchy, in general, tends to lend itself toward war as a natural state of being. Patriarchy appears not able to function properly unless it has something to fight against and dominate.

Patriarchy is a denial of nature as a rule, based on an appeal to a sense of order via the means of dominance over, rather than harmony with it. Because the Earth represents the archetype of the Divine Mother and has been worshipped in what has come to be known as ancient pagan or pantheistic religions, the world's Western monotheistic religions have unfortunately also historically treated the Divine Feminine as a threat to be met with suspicion, fear, and hostility. This is essentially what the Salem witch-burnings were all about in Puritanical New England. This distrust of the Divine Feminine is visible even in today's scientific, political and economic structures. While patriarchy has harmed, and continues to harm both women and men, the burden of carrying the rejected Divine Feminine archetype has landed squarely on the shoulders of women. Women have unequivocally been the consistent victims of the abusive and misogynistic fiat of patriarchy. It is time for the men of the world to awaken to their responsibility to revive and nurture the Divine Feminine principle within them, and help the world restore the original wholeness it has rejected.

The tale of the Half-Man reminds us that patriarchy is a symptom of brokenness and estrangement from our original nature, not its summation or inevitability. Patriarchy is an abandonment of wisdom, as we know the principle of wisdom itself to be embodied in the Hellenistic feminine figure of *Sophia*. As such, it is a deep wound that is festering, and in desperate need of healing.

The tale of the Half-Man teaches us that until we are willing to recognize and accept the Divine Feminine back into our souls, we will continue to harm ourselves, each other and the earth that sustains us. We will continue to walk around thinking, feeling and talking about ourselves and our world in a half-way. We will only be able to formulate "cures" in a half-way by simply addressing half of the symptoms; unaware, unable and unwilling to look in the very places that we have rejected to find the healing we require. Awareness of the rejected components of our shadows is a necessary first step toward that ultimate healing, but until we are willing to enter into those wounded places, things will remain the same, and we will continue to limp around in the way only a half-person can.

Vasalisa and the Baba Yaga

"Fie, fie! Until now the Russian spirit wasn't to be seen or heard, but now the Russian spirit appears before my eyes, puts itself into my mouth!" This is a familiar chant of the Baba Yaga, the old witch of Russian folklore, and a phrase repeated in many of the tales where she appears. She rides in a large pestle using her giant mortar to steer her through the deep, dark forest where she abides. She lives in a spinning house held up by chicken legs and surrounded by a fence made of human bones and glowing skulls, the remains of her many victims that have had the misfortune of stumbling across her hut unwittingly, for no one can survive an encounter with the Baba Yaga unless they are prepared to. The Baba Yaga demands conscious awareness of one's motives, desires and unconscious shadows for one to survive an encounter with her. Those who are either naïve or culpably ignorant are doomed to find their own skull on one of the many pikes surrounding her hut.

The Baba Yaga is a central fixture in many Russian fairy tales as a powerful witch, taking an ominous tone as she straddles the line between terrifying specter of death and wisdom guide. The Baba Yaga is the shared antagonist/wisdom-figure for the following stories of *Vasalisa* and *Ivan*. She is the dragon that wakes us up and forces us to integrate both the feminine and masculine energies within us. Having access to wisdom from both places is necessary in order for one to survive an encounter with the Baba Yaga. This requires a journey, and the existence of the Baba Yaga in the deep, dark woods reminds us that these journeys are not safe. Something must be confronted in the shadowy places where things creep and crawl; where the Baba Yaga's power reigns supreme. Both Vasalisa and Ivan have an important task ahead of them to claim their birthrights. Neither Ivan nor Vasalisa choose the adventures they are about to set out on, nor do they have any awareness, other than a vague sense of danger, of what they are about to encounter. They are reluctant heroes. Circumstances push them into these stories, and they begin their journeys, as most of us do, unconsciously.

We begin with the story of Vasalisa. Vasalisa is at the mercy of her wicked stepmother and stepsisters. The stepmother sends Vasalisa on an impossible task. All the light has been extinguished from their house (later discovered to be a spell that the stepmother intentionally put on the house as a way to get rid of Vasalisa, whom she hates). She instructs Vasalisa to travel into the dark wood to find the hut of the Baba Yaga and request a light that she can return home with and restore to the house. Vasalisa knows that she is headed toward her death, but she obeys her stepmother's request, nonetheless. Vasalisa feels the pull of fate, but she has not yet met her destiny, nor is she aware of it, when she sets off on her journey. She believes she is heading toward her death. It is through her own naiveté and sense of obedience to her stepmother, that she reluctantly consents to go, but an impetus to complete the journey will come from within herself later on. She must, however, consent to her own death before she can discover her true purpose and destiny.

When Vasalisa finally encounters the Baba Yaga, the witch employs her to do impossible tasks around her hut to avoid being killed and eaten by her each day. Vasalisa knows better than to try to defy her orders or to escape, either one being a death sentence for her. Instead, Vasalisa draws strength from her real mother, who had passed away long ago, but whose spirit is embodied in the form of a little doll that Vasalisa carries with her, originally a gift from her mother. The doll, who can come to life when Vasalisa is most in need, completes all the tasks that Vasalisa alone would never have been able to complete on her own. When the Baba Yaga returns to her hut each night, she is expecting Vasalisa to have failed in her tasks, thereby rewarding herself with a good meal. Each night the Baba Yaga is surprised and dismayed to discover that Vasalisa has completed all her tasks perfectly. Begrudgingly, the Baba Yaga allows her to live for one more day, and this cycle repeats itself for several days.

Vasalisa, having at last earned the Baba Yaga's respect, is eventually allowed to go home. The Baba Yaga presents her with a gift of light to bring back to her family in the form of one of the human skulls that gives off that sinister luminescent glow from within it. This becomes Vasalisa's birthright (or part of it). She does bring it back to her stepmother's house where the light itself proceeds to consume her stepmother and stepsister's whole. They can no longer terrorize and torture Vasalisa. In this moment, Vasalisa walks fully into her own strength and power. Psychologically speaking, she has dethroned the wicked stepmother and stepsister principles within her that kept her from recognizing her true worth. They had represented Vasalisa's sense of shame and her own inadequacy. Now that she realizes that she is a capable adult, she can no longer live in the stepmother's house. She must make a home for herself. It is time for her to grow up and accept her birthright.

It was by accepting and internalizing both the strength and compassion of her mother's spirit, along with the terrible power of the great witch, Baba Yaga, that Vasalisa accomplishes the task of claiming her birthright. She must internalize the powers of both in order to accomplish this. If she had made the mistake of trying to kill, or run away from the Baba Yaga, her fate would have been no different from those whose bones littered the ground around the Baba Yaga's hut. Vasalisa must now take responsibility for this terrible power she has acquired in the gift given to her by the Baba Yaga, alongside the humble strength of the kindness and wisdom embodied in the spirit of her birth mother. These two powers must learn to work together in a paradoxical tension for Vasalisa to live fully into her own wisdom and consciousness. Her birthright is her ability to acknowledge and accept that she is now a capable adult. Vasalisa discovers the wisdom of both masculine and feminine power working together to provide her with the confidence to accept her own fate and destiny.

Ivan and the Firebird

We now move on to the story of Ivan. Ivan is the son of a merchant. His mother has passed away, and when Ivan grows into adolescence, his father remarries. Because Ivan is full-grown and tall in stature, his stepmother falls in love with him. Ivan is also a fisherman, and during one of his fishing expeditions at sea, he finds himself surrounded by an entourage of thirty ships accompanying the vessel of the Tsar-Maiden from across the sea. Ivan agrees to meet with her on her ship, and they instantly fall in love with each other, deciding to marry as soon as possible. Plans are made to meet each other here at this exact spot on the sea the very next day.

Ivan's stepmother is not unaware of his rendezvous with the Tsar-Maiden, being secretly in love with him. In her jealousy, she instructs Ivan's mentor to stick a magical pin in his clothes that will cause him to fall asleep on his voyage to meet the Tsar-Maiden at sea the next day. As long as the pin remains attached to him, he cannot be woken. The mentor does as he is instructed. On the first trip back to sea, Ivan is unable to be awakened, and the Tsar-Maiden leaves his ship, resolving to try to meet him one more time the next day. The same scenario repeats itself the following day, with the mentor removing the pin from Ivan's clothes just as the Tsar-Maiden's ships are far away, enough for Ivan's call to not be heard by them. The Tsar-Maiden, aware that Ivan's mentor has been sabotaging him under the guidance of his stepmother, leaves Ivan a note alerting him to this treachery. In the note, he is also instructed to search for the Tsar-Maiden far across the sea in the *thrice-tenth kingdom*. Upon reading the note, Ivan kills his mentor for his treachery and sets off to find his beloved in the thrice-tenth kingdom.

During Ivan's adventures, he encounters the Baba Yaga residing in her ominous hut perched, aloft the sickly giant chicken legs, to whom he asks guidance to help him find the thrice-tenth kingdom. The Baba Yaga puts him off and instructs him to seek out her middle sister, who may know the way. The middle sister puts him off as well, and instructs him to seek out the youngest sister, but issues Ivan a warning. She states, "If she gets angry with you and wants to eat you, take three horns from her and ask to play on them.

Play the first horn not too loudly, the second one louder, and the third one even louder."

Ivan sets out to find the youngest of the Baba Yaga's siblings and does as he is instructed, upon discovering that the youngest Baba Yaga appears very agitated by his presence in a way the previous two had not. Upon playing the third horn as loud as he possibly can, a Firebird suddenly appears in the sky swooping down toward him. He is instructed by the Firebird to climb on its back quickly, before the hungry young Baba Yaga can grab him to cook him up for supper. Ivan and the Firebird barely escape, as the young Baba Yaga only manages to clutch and pluck out several of the Firebird's tail feathers as it bears Ivan high above the Baba Yaga's dark forest.

The Firebird bears Ivan on its back many miles before landing gently on the shores of a vast sea. The Firebird reveals to Ivan that the thrice-tenth kingdom may be found on the other side of the sea. The Firebird, however, is too tired to make the journey and can no longer bear Ivan on its back. The Firebird bids farewell to Ivan and flies off. Ivan walks along the shore until discovering a small house. Inside is an elderly woman who feeds him, and he asks her about the Tsar-Maiden and the thrice-tenth kingdom. The woman informs Ivan that the Tsar-Maiden has fallen out of love with him, and that the love she once had for him has been hidden far away.

Ivan is kept hidden and safe inside the elderly woman's small house, for she fears that if Tsar-Maiden or any of her friends should find him, that, in their grief and anger that their Maiden was rejected by Ivan, they would tear him apart. The elderly woman's daughter is a friend of the Tsar-Maiden and is able to discover from her mother that the Tsar-Maiden's love for Ivan has been hidden inside an oak tree on the other side of the sea. She reveals, "…in the oak tree is a chest, in the chest a hare, in the hare a duck, in the duck an egg, and in that egg is the Tsar-Maiden's love!"

Ivan sets out on his final quest to retrieve the Tsar-Maiden's love, hidden in that egg. He is able to successfully retrieve it and return it to the elderly woman's house, as he was instructed by her to do. That day, the Tsar-Maiden, accompanied by her thirty hosts, fly to the elderly woman's house from across the sea. The elderly woman cooks each member of the host some eggs for a meal, but the egg that the Tsar-Maiden receives holds the contents of her love for Ivan that she had buried away. Upon eating it, her love for Ivan returns. Ivan presents himself to her and they embrace each other in deep love and reconciliation. The Divine Feminine and the Divine Masculine energies have been reunited in divine union.

Vasalisa represents that Divine Feminine principle that must be balanced by the Divine Masculine, and in turn Ivan represents the Divine Masculine principle that must be balanced by the Divine Feminine. It is important to recognize that both stories and both characters belong to all of us and are being played out within our psyches all of the time. We all carry within us some version of both Vasalisa and Ivan.

Each tale features individuals who must face certain tasks and trials initiated by the dragon-like Baba Yaga in order to discover their own strength and receive their birthrights as adults, both capable of courage and discernment. The very thing each of them need resides within them, and it is only under the tests of the Baba Yaga that they become aware of what they are really capable of. Be it the bearing of light in the form of a torch, fashioned from a skull or the summoning of the Firebird, both Vasalisa and Ivan must discover what strength and courage has been hidden inside of them. Each of them encounters a moment of crisis that pushes them out of the comfort of their lives and sets them on a quest. What had formerly seemed impossible tasks doomed to end in failure or death instead became the defining moments of their lives. Both the Divine Feminine and Divine Masculine must be put to the test if they are to be awakened to emerge in our lives fully.

Impossible tasks appear to be a universal theme when faced with the challenge of transformative growth. This is why they appear as dragons to us, because they appear impossibly formidable. The Baba Yaga is always depicted as a terrifying specter, the clutches of whom no woman or man can overcome. The threat of death is almost certain, and the possibility of escape is a fool's errand. So, it is with many important paradigm-shifts that we are required to make throughout our lives. The threat of the new thing that is supposed to emerge inside of us brings us face to face with our death. What is really happening is that we are facing the extinction of the attachments we have confused our identities with for long periods of time. The Baba Yaga brings us face to face with the right death at the right time. She is most certainly dragon-like; the arbiter of fate and the trouble that fate brings with it.

When entering these deep, dark woods, where we leave behind all that is familiar, we feel as though our end is near. It is typically when we feel as though we have no other choice that we consent to walk forward into that great unknown. We instinctively know that we are leaving behind the safe bounds of comfort and familiarity. We feel cast out of our various gardens of innocence as we wander into the deep, dark woods of unknowing. There, in those old, dark forests, is where we meet the Baba Yaga. There is where we meet our death, and we must be wise about it, for our resurrection depends upon our wisdom, wit, and self-awareness.

No small amount of humility is required when confronting the Baba Yaga. Relying exclusively on our ego, our willpower, or any other form of hubris we may choose to try and overpower the Baba Yaga is a sure death sentence. So too, is chronic indecisiveness. Many sad souls find themselves trapped indefinitely in Baba Yaga's hut, as they grow old in their bones, but never grow in their spirit. Eventually these people become hollow shells of themselves. They are slowly devoured over time until there is nothing left but skull and bones, to which the Baba Yaga puts on pikes to surround her house. The Baba Yaga's hut is a monument to her cunning ability to rob those of their lives, should they willingly offer themselves to her. If we are not sobered by this thought, we ought to be...

Both Vasalisa and Ivan find themselves on a quest where they are forced to learn to cultivate the opposites to successfully accomplish their heroic tasks. Both must discover an unconscious feminine and masculine quality of themselves, that must be purposefully and consciously employed at the right time and for the right reasons. They each rely on the wisdom of some sort of totem or spirit animal to tease out of them what they need to be successful in each task. These totemic figures in the story are unrecognized, self-assured parts of each of themselves. They appear outwardly, at first, as mentors and guides, but they are each a part of Ivan and Vasalisa. When the power that these figures bring to them becomes fully recognized within them, they disappear as outer guides.

The characters of Vasalisa and Ivan are both representatives of the feminine and masculine archetypes made manifest in the soul. Both characters belong to all of us as all of us are called upon to nurture both masculine and feminine energies within ourselves. We should not forget that the Baba Yaga belongs to us as well. She is the dragon in the story that Ivan and Vasalisa must confront to grow up and become fully embodied adults. She is the "necessary evil" to instigate the quest for inner transformation and wholeness, for it is only when we discover that something is wrong that we feel emboldened to take the quests that are necessary for us to reawaken ourselves to our inner wholeness.

It is through the delicate balance of the tension between will and surrender that we discover what we need to claim our birthrights and successfully accomplish what was formerly an impossible task for us. We cannot do this without our acceptance of death as a part of life. Death is what breaks the spell of impossibility. The wisdom of Sophia, the wisdom from the Divine Feminine, who resurrects death back into our awareness, reminds us that there is *a time for everything under the sun*. Conversely, this also means that there is a time for everything to end as well. It is time for us to heal the great wounds of the West by inviting the wisdom of the Divine Feminine back in. She holds our medicine, but we must make the choice as to whether to accept it or not.

Fear is an ever-present companion on these kinds of journeys. It is the awareness of our fears that allow the gift of courage to arise inside of us. Courage is not for the already emboldened heart. Courage exists for the heart that needs it most, the heart suffering from great fear and insecurity. Fear need not be a dragon for us to have to slay, either. Rather, it can be a necessary companion that must accompany us on our journeys, while we also learn to harness it well, so it does not overcome and possess us. Fear is the necessary dragon to teach us courage. All too easily, however, we allow our fears to become more powerful than they need to be. It is one thing for fear to grip the hearts of individual people, and another thing entirely for fear to grip the hearts of communities, institutions, and entire nations. Fear can become an accepted status quo of our lives. Fear, if we allow it, can become something so pathologically imbalanced and consuming that it destroys all tensions we must learn to balance in our own lives.

When fear becomes this ingrained, reified, and institutionalized, it turns into something utterly destructive. It is the singular threat that prevents us, if we allow it, to explore our human shadows. These shadows, however, are important for us know about out, as well as to learn how to explore. This is the place where our dragons come from. This is the place where we not only learn about the parts of ourselves that we do not wish to see, but also parts of ourselves that contain great treasure and internal resources that we have not allowed ourselves, as yet, to recognize and employ. Learning the language of our shadows can help us learn to tame the dragons that are sent to us from these places, so that we begin to explore with courage, what we have not yet dared to touch. If we do not learn however, to engage with our shadows, we grow unbalanced, and this is always a recipe for more trouble.

Chapter 7
The Human Shadow: A Dragon's Den

Carl Jung, the renowned Swiss psychiatrist, coined a modern term to convey a very ancient idea. For Jung, the *Shadow* represents all the parts of ourselves that lie hidden from conscious view that we ignore or repress in some way. The shadow appears to us as an antithesis to our ego, which drives our waking consciousness, promoting the identity that we have chosen for ourselves at the expense of all other parts that do not fit into the ego's ideal. Naturally, then, the contents of our shadows reside in what Jung calls our *unconscious*.

Learning how to spend time exploring our shadows is essential for our own growth. This is the region of our psyches that produce the dragons we must face. Our Western heritage has been promoting the glorification of our ego-ideals at the expense of our shadows, assuring our continued neglect and hostility toward them.

The shadow is a metaphor, as all language is metaphor, to describe a human experience that is nonetheless very real. We not only have blind spots, personal assumptions, and biases, but we also carry within us dormant parts of our personality that may only get triggered under certain circumstances. They can surprise us when they appear, and not always in a pleasant way. Jung recognized that there are much deeper layers to us as human beings than what our everyday, conscious minds are aware of, and he worked his entire life to learn how to teach himself and others to unearth those contents of the unconscious and bring them into awareness.

Although, characterized as a kind of antagonist to the values and ideals that we identify with our conscious selves, Jung did not necessarily equate the shadow with evil. While the shadow could carry unwanted aspects of our personality that we did not like or deemed harmful, it also carried untapped potential that was ours to discover and make use of. When we do not acknowledge our shadows, we become sick and unbalanced. Our shadows then, act out unconsciously, and this is when they are most likely to become destructive. When we are acting unconsciously, our shadows become dangerous and bear the potential for evil, because they take on an autonomous nature and act through us in ways that we are unaware of. Hence, one's task is to learn to acknowledge and allow one's shadow to have a place in the internal economy of the Self. Encounter or experience in this case, rather than neglect or hostility, is the key to preventing something that resides in our shadow selves from becoming destructive.

Jung understood that the ego's existence along with its function, by necessity, creates an inevitable conflict with an individual's unconscious. The ego is the great protector of the status quo. This conflict between our ego-ideal and our shadow is what produces the dragons we are meant to face as we move through our lives. This conflict also produces the experience of *projection,* which is how the shadow aspects of our personalities "act out," when they are not consciously realized and embraced. Jung states, "The shadow is a living part of the personality and therefore wants to live with it in some form. It cannot be argued out of existence or rationalized into harmlessness."[xii]

Our shadows begin to bother us when they are neglected for too long. We will typically not have any awareness of our own shadow until it produces an intolerable, internal disruption that we are forced to acknowledge and deal with. These moments are often triggered by outward events that disturb the orderly illusions of our delicate ego-ideals, just enough to launch most of us out of the nests of our own innocence and into the unknown. Wholeness requires deeper levels of awareness, and to do that, we must be relieved of our innocence. In other words, it is typically a wounding or disorienting event; something that jolts us out of the bubble of our comfort zone, complacency, or status quo that instigates the journey of discovery into our own shadows. Our job, then, is to learn how to transform this experience into a process of radical curiosity, which then leads to the potential for healing, internal reconciliation, and wholeness. Our shadows hold the keys to our healing and wholeness.

Disrupting that internal status quo is, predictably, a disorienting experience, as is our first experiences with true wholeness itself. It can feel, at first, as though we are being torn apart. The reality is that our ego-ideals *are* being torn apart. In Buddhist terms, this phenomenon is understood as the illusory *identity*, or ego-attachment, that we have confused ourselves with, now breaking apart and falling away. For Buddhists, this is how one begins to experience enlightenment. It is these painful and disorienting events disrupting our ego-ideals that make us aware that there is more going on behind the scenes within our psyches than we know about, and as soon as we become aware of that fact, we become responsible for that knowledge. The unconscious parts of ourselves are looking for opportunities to make themselves known. Often, it takes an ego-shattering event for us to finally listen to what they have to say.

The Dragon's Den

Our unconscious selves are teeming with life and energy, and our shadows are dens for dragon's sitting on a pile of golden treasure. This shadow realm is where our dragons come from. Joseph Campbell writes, "The disgusting and rejected frog or dragon of the fairy tale brings up the sun ball in its mouth; for the frog, the serpent, the rejected one, is the representative of that unconscious deep."[xiii] The very thing that repels us in our psyche is the thing that is most likely to provide the antidote we need for healing, that we cannot obtain any other way. We are not able to receive the treasure from that which appears to us as ugly, until we learn how to acknowledge and even embrace the ugly parts.

Going back to the imagery provided for us from the story of the Lambton worm, one will recall that the dragon that young John found was cast down into a deep, dark pit. The psychological imagery is clear that this is John's shadow, where he first discovered his dragon, and to which he quickly banished it back to. If we are not cultivating the wisdom, compassion, and courage necessary to acknowledge our own dragons, then we can expect to greet them in the exact same way that John did. One will recall that John fled from his shadow by escaping into a sudden religious zeal and piety, symbolized by his journey to the Holy Land. It was not the love of wisdom and an earnest search for virtue, as such, that first instigated this journey for John. It was his attempt to make amends for the existence of his dragon in the hopes that doing so would prevent him from ever having to see it again. It was the fear of seeing himself in the eyes of the dragon, and his desire to deny this awareness completely, which initially motivated John to reform himself.

There is nothing wrong, per se, with that way of beginning our journeys, provided we eventually understand that we will come face to face with our dragons again, and if we wish to claim our birthrights, we must acknowledge their existence and be willing to strike a peaceful truce. The journey into awareness for John, was instigated by his flight from his own shadow, which as we have read, came back to greet him when he returned home. The dragon ignored, became large, dangerous, and destructive in John's unexamined and abandoned shadow. John's response to his dragon is no different than most of us when we see ours for the very first time. Even if we abandon our dragons to the depths, only to discover them resurfacing in more monstrous ways many years later, we are still faced with the choice to befriend them or fight them.

These journeys into the shadows are fundamentally necessary for us to reclaim our original wholeness. They hold important aspects of who we are and who we are destined to be, that cannot be found in any other place. We may have to sacrifice whatever ego-ideal we have been protecting for ourselves in order to reclaim the lost and hidden treasures that exist down there, but our only hope of re-discovering our inner wholeness with conscious awareness does not offer us any other short-cuts, possibilities or even reprieve from these frightening journeys into the soul. We must be willing to let go of something smaller, before we can embrace something larger.

The existence of our shadows is not, in and of itself, a problem to be solved. The problem arises in the kind of relationship we choose to have with our shadows. If we do not have both, courage and wisdom, when we approach these unexamined parts of us, we will succumb to both fear and wrath upon meeting our dragons. We cannot discover the pile of golden treasure we are meant to reclaim without first agreeing to confront the dragon that is protecting it for us. If we greet that dragon with hostility it will not yield its treasure to us, because we are not ready to receive it. If we begin to act out of our own greed for that treasure, we will project that greed onto the dragon, and the dragon will become the greed we are projecting. When we approach a dragon this way, we can expect it to attack us in an effort to protect that treasure from us. We must make peace with our dragons to receive our treasure with humility and grace. Our dragons will not yield to a truce until we do, and they will remain our antagonists for as long as we decide that they must.

When we pursue our natural gifts by trying to possess them, then those gifts will elude us or backfire on us. Claiming our natural gifts is a matter of accepting them with gratitude, not stealing them away in our own greed. That is what the inflated ego attempts to do, so it can control those gifts and force them to correspond to the ideal self-image it is protecting for us. Our shadows, however, do not conform to the mandates of our egos, however we have assembled them. We need a different part of ourselves to receive those gifts with gratitude for what they are, not for what our ego-ideal would like them to be.

Those gifts are ever-present to us but trying to take them by force is to commit an act of violence against ourselves. We begin with the assumption that we are already unworthy of that treasure, and so the only way we can obtain it is to steal it. When we fail to see our treasure as a gift to receive humbly, we miss the opportunity to receive those gifts with all their wisdom. Once we understand that the dragon's job is to guard that treasure for us until we are ready to receive it with grace and humility, then our relationship to the dragon changes. Once we stop fighting the dragon, we are ready to make peace with ourselves and accept the gift that the dragon has been protecting for us. It is then, and only then, that the dragon becomes our friend, mentor, and protector rather than our fierce enemy.

Releasing our will to power and domination is the only way we come to know and accept our own internal gold and let it live and shine through us. This is not only a challenging task for us individually; we have a rather formidable collective task in front of us to unlearn much of what we have already assumed, in our Western myths, to be the nature of all dragons.

There are many reasons why our Western minds are geared toward assault rather than acceptance of the shadow and the dragons that are born there. We have been taught to fear our shadows, to avoid them at all costs, and if failing that, cast them out like demons. This attitude toward our shadows is present within the modern economics that form the basis for so much of our political structures and allegiances. It is also present within the Enlightenment ideals of Social Darwinism, and its imperialistic ethical imperatives. It was present in Augustine's conception of his doctrine of *original sin* and Calvin's doctrine of *total depravity*. Fear of the human shadow is what informed the nineteenth century *Protestant work ethic*, most well-known for its sentiment, "Idle hands are the devil's tools." According to this doctrine, keeping busy, while not a cure for our supposed sinful nature, is designed to keep it reigned in as much as possible, by avoiding it at all costs.

In addition to these cultural biases against the apprehension of one's shadow, we have the inner struggle of the individual having to come to terms with the shadow self, as it forms the necessary opposite to the ideals of the ego self. Our instinct is to want to pretend that the shadow does not exist. This, however, only makes the pressure that our shadows put upon us more intense. John Sanford writes that, "Denial of the Shadow does not solve 'this' problem but simply makes it worse. Not only do we then lose contact with the positive aspects of this dark side of ourselves, but we will also very likely project this dark side onto other people."[xiv]

Rather than learning to acknowledge our shadows, we have cultivated practices and rituals designed to avoid them at any cost. We have so confused our shadows with dark, evil forces or a perceived "fallen" human nature, that we have cultivated nothing but fear and contempt for them and for ourselves. Add the threat of eternal damnation, should one succumb to their sinful nature by acknowledging their own shadow, and one begins to understand how Western people have developed not just a distrust, but an outright hostility toward the human shadow, and the dragons it produces. Sanford again reminds us that part of our resistance to confronting our shadows is, "The fear that if we recognize the Shadow it will overcome us... In practice, it is exactly the opposite way: we are much more likely to be overcome by the Shadow when we do not recognize it, for the unrecognized Shadow has myriad ways of asserting itself."[xv]

Fear, again, is a powerful force in our lives, and it is the primary resistance we face when doing shadow work. When the unrecognized, rejected, and undealt-with shadow begins to act out, we find ourselves at war with ourselves and at war with each other. This undealt-with fear is then what becomes responsible for much of the evil we see and experience in the world around us. If we confuse threats to our ego-ideal projections of ourselves as *only* evil, then we will continue to feed our fears by projecting evil onto others. We will also commit acts of evil as we continue to attack our shadow-projections on those we have attached them to.

Human nature is dynamic and complex, and recognizing this reality is troublesome for many of us. We all carry both light and dark within us. We all carry the capacity to do good or to do harm. Making sweeping generalizations about human nature as inevitably and only dark—helpless to produce anything of virtue—we evade the full truth of our nature, and we create excuses for not embracing and taking responsibility for it. Likewise, if we only recognize what we consider to be the positive, or light-centric aspects of our human nature, thereby denying our darkness, we also fail in our task to take responsibility for who we are. In human psychology, we have been able to observe that people rise to the expectations that are set for them. If the expectation is to enact virtue, kindness, strength, courage, and integrity, given that people have a safe enough environment to do so, then they are likely to rise to that expectation. Conversely, if our expectations of ourselves and others are that we are weak, bad, incapable, and untrustworthy, then we will rise to that expectation as well. Therefore, how we talk about ourselves and treat both our capacities for shadow and light are so important. It sets the tone for the kind of relationship we are going to have with our light and our dark.

Perfection is not what defines worth or even our wholeness. No one is perfect. That should not be something to lament, an excuse to belittle ourselves and others, or an invitation to subscribe to extreme forms of asceticism to achieve worthiness, be it to oneself or to God. Neither is an acceptance of our human nature a justification for licentiousness or evil. That too, would be a woeful failure to balance the tensions of the paradox by choosing consciously to become possessed by our own shadows. Human brokenness is not a fixed, natural state. It is a symptom of broken relationships within ourselves and between each other. Both virtue and evil have social components to them, and which one we produce largely depends on the nature of the relationship we choose to have within ourselves, and with others as well. It is possible for brokenness to be attended to and repaired through human reconciliation and grace. Brokenness is meant to be healed. Wholeness is meant to be restored. It is our original state.

We have a responsibility to retrieve, with awareness, the fullness of who we are, and these journeys into our shadows exist to encourage us to embrace the fullness of our nature, not reject it. Just because the work may prove itself to be difficult, confusing and even frightening at times, does not mean that it is evil or corrupt. When we let go of the need to be perfect, we find ourselves better-equipped to explore our shadows with more curiosity and less inhibition. Mistakes, rather than evidence of our own internal brokenness, can provide us with important opportunities for learning and growth. If we cannot accept our own fallibility, we stand no chance of learning anything from our missteps. We bypass the gift of the lessons our mistakes must teach us if we cannot allow them to. We are also unlikely to see ourselves as worthy of the wisdom that resides in our own hearts, especially if we have been taught all our lives that there is none.

The work we are intended to do as human beings is neither meant to fill-in missing parts of us, nor is it meant to punish us with "the doom of toil." Rather, that work reflects the deepest longings of our soul, which are always wooing us back to rediscover the fullness of who we already are. Piety may be a way for someone to work toward the achievement of worthiness, but that is not what the work of wholeness is about. The work of wholeness begins with the premise that you and I are already worthy, by virtue of our humanity, even if we choose to reject our own worthiness. In many ways, personal piety is the religious version of the self-help movement. Both operate under the assumption that we are "not enough" as we are, and that we need to be doing many things to make ourselves worthy or good enough, be it for God's sake, for ourselves or for others.

Wholeness tells a radically different story about us. Surrendering to our own wholeness is the hero's journey to reclaim what we have lost, as we have moved out of innocence, through inner fragmentation and into awareness; our birthrights. Those birthrights were lost to us as we went through the various turmoils of our youth, when we were too vulnerable to know how to defend ourselves against all the expectations and projections everyone else imposed on us; not developmentally mature enough yet to know how to hold all those expectations in tension with the purpose of our own souls. The fact that we are prone to distraction, confusion, and human error in this life is not evidence of a fallen state of being. It may be evidence of a frailty that is common to all of us, but not a state of ontological brokenness.

The hero's journey is an awakening to all the wonderful things that make us who we are as we grow to accept and embody them. Redemption, from this point of view, is not the pursuit of becoming who we are not, but embracing the reality of who and what we already are. Reconciliation involves not a cure for our natural state of being, but rather returning to it with conscious awareness and new wisdom. Michael Meade writes that, "The ancient tale of the soul and its divine companion present the "fall" as a necessary forgetting rather than a moral transgression or primal violation... Rather than a punishment for some original misdeed, the primary purpose of suffering in this world then becomes the labor pains needed to break open the divine seed set within the soul and recover the primary agreement that unites one world with the other."[xvi]

When we accept one end of the paradoxical tension, while rejecting the other, we get into trouble. We are more likely to sanction harm against ourselves and others, because we cannot tolerate the often difficult and complex tensions between meeting our own needs, the needs of our ego-ideals, and the needs of others. When we confront our shadows, we are learning how to carry paradoxical tensions. If, taking a cue from Buddhist philosophy, we have within our human nature, both the capacity for light and dark, then our relationship to both of those things and how we greet them is a crucial component to recognizing our wholeness and inherent worth. We should always be wary of dualisms that compel us toward continual war with our human nature, actively preventing us from recognizing and taking responsibility for our own wholeness.

Because this kind of thinking is so ingrained in our very cultural fabric, we automatically set up opposing opposites in our daily lives that we are not even aware of. I use the term "opposing opposites" intentionally, because as we have already discovered, not all opposites are meant to be in opposition to each other. It never occurs to us, unless the status quo gets disrupted enough, that the manifestation of opposites presents us with a tension that we must pay attention to. The tension is a gift that provides us with the opportunity to engage in our own inner dialogue and to instigate the process of inner reconciliation. Learning how to carry more of our paradoxical tensions within us gets the ball rolling and teaches us to grow more fully into our own healing and wholeness.

The challenge of acknowledging and balancing both the light and the dark aspects of our human nature are very important in our journey to uncover everything we can learn about who we are and why we are here. As previously stated, not all that is dark is evil. Not all that is "of the flesh" is evil. Our bodies are the vehicles for our souls; our treasured thoughts, hopes, assumptions, ideals, and experiences. Our minds cannot function without the good will of our bodies. We need to love them and take care of them properly. When it comes to true spirituality, there is no divide between the mind and the body that many ancient and modern Western philosophers and theologians have surmised. This is one of the stories about ourselves that our living and emerging myths are asking us to let go of.

We need our natural curiosity to learn how to respond to the deep and profound mysteries of our own lives if we are to become open to the revelation of our original wholeness. If our shadows, and each of the human resistances we experience are to be understood as merely symptoms of a fallen nature, then we have no reason to cultivate the curiosity necessary to explore them, because our nature by this definition, stays statically and irrevocably malevolent. Our nature is much more dynamic than that. It is certainly not something we need to be saved from. We need a method and a language with which to learn to greet our resistances with compassion and curiosity, trusting that they are a necessary part of how we retrieve the knowledge of our original wholeness.

Doing our shadow work is very important and necessary for the process of wholeness to unfold. Through this work, we not only learn what is most important for us to learn about ourselves, but we also learn to distinguish between what is troubling to us (and about us) and what is evil. Without shadow work, those two things all too easily get confused with each other.

As noted previously, fear is a powerful dragon that must be tamed before it does produce evil. Greed is another such untamed dragon. It manifests as a domineering will for power over others. Evil is often produced by those who have become possessed by greed and other aspects of their shadow selves. The thirst for power is something that we are all vulnerable to, particularly if we are feeling powerless in our lives. Before we demonize the phenomenon of power too quickly, however, we need to recognize that our need for power also requires a balance. There are many situations in our lives where the cultivation and use of power works for our benefit as well as the benefit of others, just as there are plenty of situations where power absolutely corrupts and destroys.

If we become consumed by power (which would mean resolving the paradoxical tension by becoming possessed by power), then that power turns into a will to dominate others with brutality and indifference. Wherever there is a perceived need for a power structure, the temptation to abuse that power exists. Ignorance and indifference on our part is also what allows evil to exist. Evil gets perpetuated all the time by all of us through our own ignorance of, and indifference toward, it. It is not too difficult to see how the evil in the hearts of individuals possessed by greed and having a gift for charismatic group manipulation can produce systemic evils that all of us eventually become culpable for, either knowingly or unknowingly.

On a psychological level, I believe that it is entirely possible for one to give oneself over to their shadow and become possessed by it, thereby abandoning the balance required of wholeness. This becomes another opportunity for evil to take root in the heart of a human being. The manifestation of evil in the human heart, at least in part, appears as a symptom of a failure to balance the internal tensions of the shadow personality and the ego personality. John Sanford states, "Both repression of the knowledge of the Shadow, and identification with the Shadow, are attempts to escape the tension of the opposites within ourselves... The motive, of course, is to escape the pain of the problem, but if escaping the pain leads to psychological disaster, carrying the pain may give the possibility for wholeness."[xvii]

If we can transcend the punishing dualisms that prevent us from exploring our shadows, then we stand to be recipients of their great wisdom. It is only in the shadows that we discover what we are truly capable of, for both good and ill. We cannot afford to neglect our own shadows. The risks are too severe to us and to others, and we can see what is happening to our world today due to our failure to confront both our individual and collective shadows.

Resistance toward our shadows is one thing, but outright hostility is another. Resistance can be worked with and transcended. Hostility does not lend itself to such treatment because it has already consented to war and fortified its position. The kind of relationship we are capable of having, and choose to have, with our shadows sets the tone for how we will regard ourselves as well as others. Shadow work is about much more than introspective curiosity. It has everything to do with our capacity to relate to ourselves and others with grace, curiosity, compassion, and wisdom. Our ability (or lack thereof) to work with our own shadows has consequences for the outer world around us.

The Creativity of the Dark

One part about our shadows that must not be overlooked is the depth of creativity they contain. One has only to pay attention to one's own dreams to know the truth of this. The kinds of images that our unconscious produces and sends our way during dreams, deep meditation or active imagination exercises can be truly extraordinary, if sometimes disturbing. Since our ego is the waking part of ourselves that sorts and interprets information about us and our world in very specific ways, it is limited in its ability to think outside of its own box. Our shadows can provide us with a brand-new way of looking at things and even solving problems, provided we have given them voice and learned to listen to them; granting the dragons and other creatures they send our way a viable place in our psyche.

When we allow ourselves to incorporate the wisdom of our shadows into our waking lives, they become more vibrant and creative as well. We find ourselves not only imbued with new wisdom, but new purpose as well. We discover what our souls were intended for in this life and on this planet. When we set a place at the table for our dragons, we benefit from the wisdom they now have to share with us. Our dragons carry elements of *The Fire That Never Dies* within them, which gives us access to that Fire more often and in smaller doses. This may mean that our need to confront that Fire less often and much more dramatically decreases over time, simply because we make doing our own soul work a regular routine, rather than a major event we find ourselves thrust into every fifteen to twenty years or so.

This creativity also allows us to maneuver the parts of ourselves, our dragons, that we are still working to befriend. It gives us more tools to know how to respond to them apart from just shame, anger and rejection when we still find ourselves struggling to reconcile with them. When we discover a part of ourselves that we do not like, and is giving us some trouble, this creativity teaches us to ask the question, "What do I need to learn about myself in this struggle?" rather than, "How can I make this part of myself go away?"

It is to our benefit, creatively, to come to terms with some part of ourselves that we are afraid of or ashamed of. Someone who acknowledges the fact, for instance, that they have the capacity to be very cruel, despite their commitment to be a person of kindness and tenderness, all of a sudden becomes aware of an energy that resides within them that they had not been aware of before. This can be an ego-crippling experience, as of course it is designed to be, especially if one likes to think of oneself as a kind person. So, what is this person to do with this new information? Knowing that one has the capacity for their own cruelty can help them be more aware of that energy and manage it in a conscious way, preventing it from unconsciously acting out on other people. When it acts out unconsciously, it almost always acts out destructively. Becoming aware of one's own capacity for cruelty may cause that person to locate the deeper source of the cruelty, which has grown out of an old wound, fear or deep sadness that is unresolved and unhealed.

In this process, one can also possibly learn when, where, and why that cruelty was born. Perhaps, it was born in a moment of experiencing someone else's cruelty. As a wise person once taught me, we all learn how to be cruel from those who have been cruel to us. When we acknowledge our capacity for such things, they no longer have any control over us, and they can also move us toward greater compassion for others, who are acting out their own cruelty toward others unconsciously. This compassion may lead to more effective ways of challenging that cruelty in others, without succumbing to our own cruelty in response to them.

When we allow ourselves to see our dark places and learn to make peace with them, we also make available to us a richness and depth that inspires new ways of thinking, seeing ourselves and the world, and sometimes skills that have been lying dormant within us that we would never have discovered, had we not been willing to enter into our shadows and see what they are holding for us. Going into our dark spaces gives us the knowledge and clarity to decipher the language of our souls, which are constantly attempting to bring into our awareness the things we need to live our lives abundantly.

The benefit of this exploration means that we return from the underworld of our lives with a renewed sense of purpose, vigor and capacity for creativity and compassion. The creativity required of us, for instance, to put our fear to work in life-giving ways rather than destructive ways, is one of the gifts of these forays into the underworld. We are always afraid that we will not survive our times in the shadows. Unfortunately, the only way to overcome that fear is to consent to going into those shadows armed only with courage. The lights of awareness that comes from our encounters with the darkness are unique to the shadow. We do not access that kind of light any other way.

Part II
Naming Our Dragons

"The idea of the dragon is rooted in a deep and universal human apprehension about our own nature and the threats presented by the universe in which we live."

~Doug Niles[xviii]

Chapter 8
Ego: The Dragon 'Fafnir'

The word *ego* is a Latin word for "I." Psychologically speaking, the ego is referred to as that aspect of the human psyche that governs waking consciousness. Sigmund Freud popularized the term *Ich,* which is the German translation for ego, as one part of a triune personality system he believed all people shared. Even if many of Freud's theories about the human personality have been rejected in modern day psychology, the term itself has remained a fixture in our modern vernacular. Everyone knows what an ego is and how it is most often used in everyday language. Again, an ego is not a real thing. There is no neuro-biological organ in the brain that corresponds to a part of us called an "ego." It is a metaphor used to describe an experience that is common to all of us. It is the part of *me* that participates in waking awareness, identifies myself as being separate and unique from other selves, and protects the status quo of my waking life.

This differentiation between "I" and "not I" is a condition of the sense of duality we have inherited in the Western Psyche. The Eastern Psyche tends to experience this much differently. According to Joseph Campbell, the concept of identity in the East is meant to "evoke in the individual the experience of identity with the universal mystery, the mystery of being. You are it. Not the 'you,' however, that you cherish. Not the 'you' that you distinguish from the other."[xix] It is because this distinction between the two traditions is so greatly pronounced that most of us in the West cannot simply pretend to be "ego-less." We must learn to treat our ego as another part of the psyche that has a rightful place within our internal economy of Self. For those of us born and bred in the West, it simply means that our path toward wholeness may look very different from those raised and nourished in Eastern traditions.

Even though the idea of the ego is widely accepted as a part of our modern vernacular, like many important concepts, it is often over-simplified or misunderstood. This tends to happen with complex ideas. When you hear someone say, "That person has a healthy ego," they could be giving them a compliment or criticizing them. When we think of someone having a "big ego," we tend to be suggesting someone may be cocky, arrogant, or full of themselves. It is true that these can all be inflated expressions of the ego, but the ego itself serves a greater purpose than one's own self-aggrandizement. It is the supreme guardian of the status quo inside of every person.

The ego is the conscious part of the Self that takes in data from the outside world every day and interprets it through whatever filter (or personal narrative) one has identified themselves with. That filter could be cocky, aggressive or arrogant, but it can also be restless, ashamed or anxious. Our egos are built to defend and reinforce the stories of ourselves we have most identified with. If we believe that we are the greatest person on earth, then that is what the ego defends and upholds. Conversely, if we believe that we are worthless, then our ego will also fiercely defend that identity as well. Our egos will look for evidence in everyday life to affirm the stories we have chosen for ourselves as true, often at the expense of whatever data or evidence contradicts the accepted narratives our ego is protecting for us.

The ego, being a fixed component of the Western psyche, like all our many parts, does serve a purpose. Therefore, it needs to be embraced with wisdom and compassion, as do all components of the psyche. It can, however, present itself as a dragon that stands between us and our ability to grow as individuals when it feels threatened or becomes inflated. Just as people can become possessed by their shadows they can also become possessed by their egos. Whenever we experience the possibility that our identity may be changing or shifting in any way, our ego is often the first part to detect and prevent it from happening and the last part to surrender to the change when it becomes necessary for us to do so.

If we understand why this happens the way it does, then we need not treat our ego as an enemy to be conquered or overcome. Like any other dragon we might face, our ability to tame the ego depends on our relationship to it. If we treat it like an enemy, we can expect it to behave like an enemy. If we can, however, recognize its value for what it can and is doing for us, then we stand a better chance at taming it and teaching it how to become more flexible. The ego's job is to protect our sense of identity, however we have assembled it, so whenever that begins to shift, the ego naturally feels threatened. Like any of our other parts, it just wants to know that it is not going to be out of a job. It needs to be nurtured into the growth process that challenges old stories and status quos that no longer serve our best interest as individuals rediscovering our inherent wholeness.

Marie-Louise von Franz writes of the importance of an ego balanced with other components of the internal eco-system of the Self. She recognizes the importance of the ego to the internal economy of the Self, while at the same time, giving us a clue as to its proper place there. Von Franz says that the ego fulfils its purpose properly if it works as a tool in line with the impulses of the self.

When we attend to the other parts of ourselves with conscious awareness and exercise their influences in our lives, we also train our egos to make way for the acceptance of new information, so they can recognize, assimilate, and protect it for us. In this way, the ego can become a partner in our continued exploration of the soul, rather than just a detractor. We can appeal to its desire to want to discover new things and take credit for them, even as we must balance the tension between the expectations of the ego-ideal and the fuller reality of the Self.

One advantage the ego does have that allows us to work with it this way, is that the ego can be very excited to discover something new, even if it tends to interpret that discovery through the rigidity of its own expectations. The ego is attracted to novelty and likes to take some credit for making new discoveries. The ego also works hard to make sense of the new information and put it in a context that it can understand. We often experience moments like this with a frenetic and excited feeling of anticipation. We now have a chance to experience something new or get to the bottom of a mystery! We enjoy moments like this, and certainly, the ego plays a part in giving us these kinds of experiences, even if we must learn to quiet it a little to make room for other components of the psyche to engage these new discoveries in different ways as well.

While the ego may initially be excited at the prospect of discovering something new, it is still often unprepared for how new information might impact its ability to protect the status quo. It is typically when the novelty of a new discovery wears off that the ego becomes fearful and protective. This is why cultivating an ability to abandon the mandates of one's ego in the middle of a new journey is so central to the hero's journey.

Most heroines and heroes begin the undertaking of a journey of transformation when starting a new adventure, though most often they are blissfully unaware of this fact. The journey begins with one expectation and ends with something entirely different. The ego helps to get us out the door, but at some point, must be abandoned for us to learn the new wisdom that our soul has set before us to learn. If the ego knew what it was getting into, we would never begin these important journeys that shape our lives in innumerably significant ways. Eventually, however, the voice of the ego must once again return to us to help us protect the new status quo that has been established as a result of a transformation that has taken place. This is how the ego plays its role in the endless cycles of birth, death, and rebirth. If we are all committed to our own personal growth throughout our lives, we will continue to repeat this cycle over and over again.

While there may be times when we bemoan the stubbornness of our egos and may be tempted to regard them as something that we wish to rid ourselves of completely, we must remember a basic principle of the human psyche, which is that we cannot get rid of any of its parts, including the ego. Wrestling with our egos is an important part of our growth work and we must honor the role it plays in that growth process.

It should not be surprising to us that this part of our personality tends to believe, often, that it is the only part that exists inside of us, and therefore often behaves as though it is. Accepting that the ego necessarily functions with a certain degree of autonomy within the psyche, only helps us understand better what gets it excited as well as what threatens it. When we are willing to engage the truth of our ego with curiosity, we no longer treat our egos as enemies to be conquered. Rather we accept them with compassion while we also exert good boundaries, as we learn to work with them wisely and appropriately.

The experience of the ego is one of a particular kind of consciousness. Once we are aware of ourselves in this way, we cannot become unaware of ourselves. Remember, that we cannot return to innocence. Our only option is to guide our egos to better interact with the other parts of our personality. This means that when the time comes for us to make a big change inside of us, we need an ability to re-purpose our egos to an emerging status quo, or new story about ourselves; one which is hopefully moving us toward greater healing, wisdom and wholeness. Failure to do this ensures that we are in for all kinds of trouble when things begin to manifest as change in our lives. A rigid resistance ensures an adversarial relationship between our ego and the rest of our internal economy, which is already resting on a tenuous truce.

It is not the presence of the ego that becomes damaging to us, but rather a rigid relationship and attachment to a particular story about us that fortifies its myopic vision of itself and the world. That, of course, does lead to problems. This is what occurs when we accept and collude with our ego's belief that it is the totality of our being, and that it is supposed to be in charge of everything. It is a collusion we are all susceptible to. It is one of the reasons why anything that comes to confront whatever status quo the ego is protecting appears to us, often enough, as a dragon.

The ego is the first part of us to notice the presence of a dragon, though it is not the one to initially carry out the quest to tame it, because the dragon appears to it only as a threat. Since the ego is trying to protect itself, its first instinct is to attempt to kill the dragon. This is why dragon-taming requires an acknowledgment of, and good relationship with, all of our parts. The ego alone is not equipped for dragon-taming. Even when we get our ego on board to learn to tame dragons, rather than fight them, we must manage its desire to want to take control of the entire dragon-taming process. Our egos must be gently guided to work with the other parts of our psyche in order to successfully greet and tame dragons.

The ego, by its own nature, is limited in its scope. Its job is to guide us successfully through our day and accomplish our numerous and varied tasks. It is only likely to seek and register information that confirms our view of ourselves and the views we have of the world. Even though we need to learn how to work with the ego, it is a necessity that we are able to transcend it from time to time, and this takes great care, compassion, and wisdom. An emotional or spiritual detachment from our egos does not therefore cause our egos to no longer exist. It means that we have altered our relationship with our egos in such a way that allows us the gift and flexibility of growth. Each of our internal cast of characters needs to know when to step up and step down, depending on their strengths and depending on the situation we find ourselves in. The same is true of the ego.

The ego is not likely to enjoy the feeling of being dethroned of such ultimate power when it becomes appropriate for it to step down, which is why we need the wisdom of a dragon-tamer over a dragon-slayer to help our egos acclimate to this change. For this reason, we must expect that the ego will at first try to defend its position, typically by trying to inflate itself. If we can exercise patience and compassion for it, however, we stand a better chance at helping it learn to be more flexible and cooperative.

Failure to do this kind of work with our egos can, and often does, lead to disaster. Because it seeks to possess knowledge by its nature, the ego can easily become greedy for the control of that knowledge. Our egos know how precious knowledge is, because knowledge is power. Knowledge, in mythology, is often likened unto treasure. In the world of alchemy, the object of the source of all knowledge and wisdom is called the *philosopher's stone*. In the Gnostic traditions, this knowledge is considered to be secretly hidden and only capable of being discovered or having its wisdom translated by only a select few individuals capable of penetrating its mysteries and discerning its wisdom. Mysteries are always intriguing to us but discovering the mysteries of hidden wisdom offers us another incentive. To have access to such knowledge makes us feel special. It makes us feel important.

The ego likes to feel special, and there is nothing more enticing to it than the possibility of discovering new or hidden knowledge that few others have access to. Just like we all relish being privy to the inside joke, or part of an exclusive club, the ego enjoys the prospect of being distinguished from others in that unique and special way. It is always on a quest to discover secret knowledge or hidden treasure. There is nothing like a good mystery and the prospect of a heightened sense of importance to entice the ego!

It is important to remember that even though this quest for hidden knowledge can quickly be overcome by greed or thirst for domineering power, at its root it is a profound awareness of, and response to, the deep mysteries of life. The philosopher's stone, the Holy Grail, and other symbols of profound mystery to be discovered, provides one with the purpose of a quest, which, as we have already indicated, is an archetypal need and desire in all of us. The true quest for the philosopher's stone, we eventually discover, is the quest for the secret, hidden knowledge of our own souls. If, however, we are not in touch with our shadows, that quest can quickly become consumed by our own greed and lust for power.

In the Nordic tale of *Fafnir*, a strong and warrior-like dwarf finds himself coveting a hoard of his father's treasure, which also contains a ring of power that has been forged by Loki. Fafnir becomes so overcome with his greed for the treasure that he kills his father and steals it. Fafnir appears to revel in his cleverness about getting away with the theft. At the same time, he becomes simultaneously possessed by a deep paranoia about the prospect of anyone trying to steal it back. This action, coupled with his lust and fear, slowly begins to turn Fafnir from a dwarf into a dragon.

Fafnir, rather than confronting and taming his own inner dragons, becomes a dragon himself, and in this way, becomes possessed by the untamed dragon present within himself. And so, he confuses his quest for knowledge and wisdom with greed and power. He becomes his own worst enemy, and in turn, becomes an enemy to all others, even his kin. He is now a slave to the ring and the power he perceives it gives him. In turn, consumed by greed and lust, he attacks and kills anyone who comes close to him, assuming that they are attempting to rob him of his treasure which he has chosen to hoard for himself, rather than share with his people. Fafnir's greed overcomes all other aspects of his personality and consumes them entirely. He can no longer hear their wisdom or pleas for charity, for he has closed himself off from them.

An inflated ego is the result of succumbing to the belief that it is the only part of us that exists, or at the very least, the only part that is important. When it feels threatened, it naturally inflates itself. All other parts of us, now rejected, are externalized and projected onto others, perceived then as threats that must be destroyed. All other parts, if they are acknowledged at all, are to be readily sacrificed if proven to be a threat to the inflated ego. If we liken the character of Fafnir in the story to an ego-inflation, or ego-possession, then we understand the consequences of such a choice. We ourselves will become closed off to any input, critique, vulnerability or any sense of gratitude, wonder or generosity, both from within ourselves and from others.

When this happens, wisdom and compassion no longer hold any place in the internal economy of the Self, as they would be a direct threat to the unquestioned power of the inflated ego. Fafnir begins as a noble, fierce, and courageous dwarf, capable of great deeds beyond even those of his brothers. When he allows himself to be manipulated, however, by the greed of the treasure he is hoarding, his good will transforms into a poisonous hatred which he then, as a dragon, breathes as fire all around him to kill anyone who might try to approach him or his beloved hoard.

The search for knowledge, insight, enlightenment or wisdom can quickly become polluted by greed and a lust for power. These then are sustained by the fear that someone else might find the mythological treasure first and exploit it for their own ends before we have our chance. Many honest inquiries into the mysteries of existence being explored in Western occult traditions, for instance, often become quests for power and domination above all else. Our entire modern, Western economy is also built on the premise of the accumulation of this power and desire for domination. The philosopher's stone, rather than a great source of wisdom to be shared with all, becomes an object of desire to hoard and protect from the perceived threat of others stealing it away. While mysteries, in and of themselves, may be life-giving, the hoarding of secret information almost always becomes destructive. If we do not do our own balancing work between the light and dark aspects of ourselves, spiritual quests transform into obsessive pursuits of power for the sake of power.

The story of Fafnir illustrates the grave seriousness that underlies any quest we set out to take, however noble it may seem to us at the time; however pure our hearts and intentions might have been at the beginning. If we do not learn to contend with the parts of our shadow selves that are vulnerable to fear and greed, then they will consume us. Fafnir traded in his wisdom for greed, when he chose to hoard the wealth he was guarding. Ironically, he does not succumb to the dragon-like parts of his personality until he chooses to become blind to them and thereby possessed by them. That is when the dragon consumes him and becomes a threat to everyone else as well.

Fafnir's transformation describes mythologically, the transformation that takes place when our ego begins to act like a cruel dictator, trying to usurp the throne of "Self," suppressing all other voices that belong to the internal economy of our psyches. We are also likely to face a similar threat, if we are not careful, when we need to repurpose our ego to protect a new story of ourselves that puts the old story at risk.

The ego's biggest fear is that whatever it is protecting is going to be stolen away, and its purpose will then cease to exist. If we collude with this fear, then we are giving all our power over to the ego to protect itself and neglect our own responsibility to help it accommodate other parts of the psyche and other stories about ourselves that they are carrying. This is why, when we need to repurpose the ego, we must spend a lot of time comforting and reassuring it that it is still valued and that we need its participation to help welcome the emerging, new stories of ourselves designed to bring us more wisdom and wholeness. For as powerful as the ego believes itself to be, it is also very fragile, and this is an important thing to remember when learning how to respond to its fears with wisdom and patience. We want and need our egos to work for us, but we must remind them continuously that they must be inclusive to other parts of our psyches, even our dragon-like parts.

Even though an ego can become very dragon-like itself, it is nonetheless a vital and important part of the human psyche. It is the part that gives us the ability to do all the various tasks in life that we are called upon to do every day. It is the part that puts the plan in motion. As such, it governs our willpower, which is only one of many different forms of power and wisdom we are meant to learn to use wisely during the courses of our lives.

This then presents the paradoxical tension we are called to attend to when we need to make a change in our lives. The will of the ego and the power of our unconscious parts create an inner tension that wakes us up and revitalizes us, preparing us for transitions in life. We need the strength of our egos, as we also need the ability to tame them appropriately. Our egos need also, to learn about the art surrender and make room for other parts of the psyche, for they provide us with their own versions of strength and fortitude, which the ego cannot provide, but which we nevertheless need.

The tale of Fafnir teaches us that we need to be paying attention or else we can become unconsciously possessed by our own fear, greed, and malice. Anytime one part of us is neglected for too long, it is likely to grow out of balance, and when this happens it becomes more susceptible to the powers that would turn it into a dragon. Our egos need to learn the art of sacrifice and surrender just as much as any other part of us does. We, as whole people, need also to learn how to use its powers effectively when we need them. Once again, we recognize the importance of balancing a paradoxical tension as we work to reawaken ourselves to our own wholeness. We will encounter resistances toward the acceptance of our wholeness along the way. These are the necessary struggles we must encounter as we grow.

Chapter 9
Resistance: "The Great and Powerful Oz"

"Pay no attention to that man behind the curtain!"
~The Great and Powerful Oz

A resistance is born when a deep longing arises in our soul that guarantees we will need to confront something beyond the boundaries of our comfort zones. Resistances are also born in unguarded moments when we may feel embarrassed, unpleasantly surprised, or seriously wounded in a way we could not anticipate or were helpless to prevent. In this way, a resistance serves to protect ourselves from the possibility of getting hurt again. We cultivate many resistances throughout our lives. Resistances can be powerful allies, but they can also become powerful dragons. We can ignore them for a time, but not forever. A resistance may not appear to us as a dragon until we are forced to come face to face with it, or decide that it is time to move forward in our lives, putting at risk our own sense of comfort and safety. The invitation to grow is simultaneously the invitation to greet resistances.

A resistance can be part of an internal warning system that alerts us to the possibility that there is something or someone to fear. It could be fear of something bad happening, fear of being taken advantage of, or harmed in some way, fear of the unknown, or fear of our own failure. It can also be the fear of growing up and moving forward in our lives, because we must leave behind the comfort of that which is familiar. Our resistances can feel *all powerful*. We often feel a sense of despair that there is anything that we can do about them once we recognize that they are standing in between us and where we want to go. It is not typically until we feel we have no other choice, that we stop ignoring our resistances and begin entertaining the idea of confronting and working through them.

The Great and Powerful Oz is what is standing between Dorothy and her ability to get back home to her small farm in Kansas. If she wants to see her home again, she has no other choice but to seek out the Wizard in hopes that his power and magic can somehow send her back. If we read the story of *The*

Wizard of Oz mythologically (which is also to read it psychologically), we may interpret all the characters in the story as different parts of Dorothy's own psyche. Some of these characters are allies and others are not. Some are explicitly dragon-like and others are simply at odds with each other. One of the reasons this story is timeless is because its characters are so archetypal. Who of us isn't familiar with our own Cowardly Lion or the rigid dogmatic qualities of a Tin Man struggling to follow his heart and discover his own bliss? Who of us hasn't experienced the confusion of a Straw Man struggling to think clearly or assert a well-informed argument? Who of us cannot relate at times to feeling lost, alone, and alienated from ourselves and our home, desperate to find a way back?

Most of us, I believe, can also identify the presence of a Great Wizard within ourselves; an all-powerful and terrifying specter, capable of both, administering power or taking it away; both providing hope or destroying it. In the movie version of this fascinating tale, the Wizard's appearance is very fearsome and dragon-like, with his green skin and sharp teeth. His fiat in the kingdom of Oz is supreme and the belief in his ability to either grant or deny a wish is so completely unquestioned, that it never occurs to anyone living in the Emerald City to resolve their own dilemmas without his guidance or blessing. Its citizens believe that they are neither powerful nor wise enough to do so on their own...or so the Great Wizard would have them all believe. We soon discover that this ruthless wizard is nothing more than *the man behind the curtain*, an old circus man who was himself stranded in the land of Oz many years ago.

So, it goes, when we finally learn to face our resistances head on and move through them, we discover that there was never a monster or an all-powerful wizard in the first place. Our resistance projected a monster or a dragon onto our imagination in order to make sense of our fear. Our resistances project dragon-like specters, also, to get our attention. The appearance of the Great Wizard was certainly a powerful projection that served to capture Dorothy's attention. Once a resistance has our attention, our task then becomes to investigate the proverbial *man behind the curtain* and learn about what wisdom he has to offer us.

Confronting a resistance does not always lead us in a straight line, and we need to be prepared for that. Sometimes there are twists and turns and unexpected detours as we learn how to confront our resistances. We also need to be prepared to fail in our attempts to confront them a few times before challenging them successfully, just as Dorothy and her companions had to do. For most of us, there is a considerable amount of testing the waters before we are fully ready to confront and move through them. They may convince us that they need to be appeased in a special way, with a magic trick or the offering of a totem of some kind. The Great Wizard sets Dorothy and her friends on an impossible task for the ultimate totem, the wicked witch's broom.

Dorothy must face her shadows before she can be granted her wish. If she is going to find her way back home, that is to say, rediscover her own wholeness consciously, she must become aware of everything that lies deep down in her unconscious. The character of the wicked witch, much like the Baba Yaga, represents the shadow side of the Divine Feminine that Dorothy must confront and integrate in order to gain access to everything that lies within her shadow. Once the wicked witch is melted by the water that Dorothy throws onto her, it cools her off and removes her fear. The outward manifestation of the witch disappears as Dorothy acknowledges and accepts her ability to wield that terrible power within herself.

Having dissolved the fearsome specter of the wicked witch, Dorothy can now incorporate her energy and power to serve her faithfully, without having to fear that power. Dorothy's encounter with the wicked witch is her first experience of her own power. She too has the ability to either create or destroy. She has even gained the respect and loyalty of all the other creatures of her shadow (the guards and the flying monkeys), previously enslaved by the wicked witch. Once the witch is destroyed, they immediately switch their allegiance to Dorothy. Having now completed this task, set forth for her by the Wizard, Dorothy is ready to greet him for a final time and claim her birthright. She has one more test to pass. She must face the terrifying specter of the Great Wizard and challenge his injustice as he attempts to deny her request to return home even after bringing him the witch's broom, per his request. She does this, and while she does this, something very interesting happens. The Great Wizard is revealed to be nothing more than the man behind the curtain.

When Dorothy and her companions discover this, their fear is instantly disarmed, and so is Dorothy's resistance. There is an important decision to be made here. Their response to the man behind the curtain is crucial. They scold him for frightening them, but they do not threaten to harm him. Had they responded only out of their anger, however justified it might have been, and killed or wounded the man, they would have lost the opportunity to receive the gifts they needed to obtain from him. They could have chosen to succumb to their anger, which would have left them carrying their resentment and fear around with them for the rest of their lives and put them at risk of perpetrating the same sins as that of the Great Wizard. Had they simply responded solely out of their own anger, they would not have been able to claim their birthrights. This moment called for a different kind of wisdom and insight.

What the man behind the curtain shows them in the end is that they already have everything they need within themselves, and that it has been there from the very beginning. This knowledge is his gift to them. The man behind the curtain has now transformed from the dragon-like wizard into a fallible wisdom figure. He was originally a *trickster* but has now been revealed. Dorothy and her friends had been unable to believe in themselves until this moment. In fact, they had so desperately needed to believe in a grand and terrible wizard to whom they might appeal for mercy, as well as favor, that they quite willingly gave all their hope (and thereby their power) over to the Great Wizard.

The Wizard was carrying the wisdom and the power they had projected onto him. The Wizard was the ultimate wish-fulfillment of the childhood fantasy of a benevolent parent, god or dictator, to whom they could appeal to for mercy and favor. The man behind the curtain is the symbol of the now accepted and integrated inner power and wisdom of each character to recognize within themselves. Now is the moment where Dorothy and her companions make conscious what was unconscious. Now is the moment when they all receive and accept what already belonged to them from the beginning.

The man behind the curtain in each of us does not reveal himself until we are ready to see him. It is not until we are able to acknowledge and accept our own power that the Wizard transforms. This is the moment when we claim our birthrights. We are now aware that the Wizard is, as are all the other characters in the story, a part of ourselves, and we begin to take responsibility for him and care for him appropriately.

The man behind the curtain is not yet done failing Dorothy, however. He has agreed to take Dorothy back home to Kansas, but ultimately leaves her in the lurch as his hot-air balloon flies away without her, claiming ignorance of the ability to control his own balloon or guide it back to pick Dorothy up once it has left the ground. Now, that he has revealed the secret of his knowledge and wisdom (or lack thereof), he is no longer the all-powerful wizard, capable of performing magic tricks and granting wishes. He is a mortal man who sometimes lacks the knowledge or skill to do everything perfectly, including keeping his balloon on the ground long enough to take Dorothy home with him. He cannot become the Wizard again. He must now disappear as an outer principle, for his power has been made an internal reality for Dorothy. Even though she has now realized her own power, there is still a part of her that wants to believe in the magical Wizard, someone who is capable of making everything all right again and take her back home. It is not to be. Some part of her still wants to hang on to this old resistance. Dorothy has one more task;

one more vital part of herself to receive and accept before she can return home. She must come face to face now, with the good witch.

The good witch is a symbol for the lighter part of the Divine Feminine that Dorothy has yet to fully claim and accept. This part represents the fully integrated ego principle, giving Dorothy access to her *own* power and will. It is through this character that she will discover the power to send herself home. She must fully abandon her desire for an outer power principle, a divine mother or divine father, symbolized by the wish-fulfillment of the Great Wizard and begin to surrender to the reality and acceptance of her own power. In this sense, the good witch presents herself to Dorothy as the embodiment of this power. It is appropriate that Dorothy learns to trust her own Divine Feminine powers to guide her home, over the outer power principle of the Great Wizard, which was a patriarchal manifestation of power. The outward father and mother figure can no longer help Dorothy. She must learn to actualize these divine energies within herself.

Dorothy does make it back home, but home is not the same and neither is Dorothy. Dorothy has awareness and power now. The innocence she initially fled by confronting her own inner turmoil, symbolized by the great twister (crisis) that sent her into Oz and initiated the quest into her own undiscovered country, is a thing of the past. She knows about Oz now. She can never un-know it. She is now responsible for everything that she learned about herself in Oz. She is responsible for each and every character she brought with her into and out of that land and is also responsible for nurturing each of them as she grows and learns more and more about herself and what she is capable of.

Each resistance we experience as a great and powerful wizard appears that way to get our attention. That is its purpose, as is the purpose of all dragons. It alerts us to the fact that there is something we need to reclaim for ourselves and something more for us to discover within us. Even if we resist, life has its way of pushing us into deeper levels of awareness anyhow. The choice to fight or to surrender to this reality is ours alone. Life, however, will send a twister to provoke us, if necessary, if we find ourselves resisting for too long.

We cannot remain complacent forever. What we discover, when we finally and decidedly walk through our resistances is the man behind the curtain; the humble voice of wisdom behind the mask of hubris, that has an important gift for us. While he lays down clues as to his true nature, he cannot simply reveal himself, at least not right away. We must seek him out, because it is only when we are ready to go on that journey and receive his gift, that he shows himself. Dorothy needed the Great and Powerful Oz to exist and protect her birthright for her until she was ready to see the man behind the curtain and claim that birthright for herself. These characters that are a part of Oz and are a part of

Dorothy, are also a part of us. They all have different voices, and all serve different purposes, but in the end, they all belong to each other.

Something arises within us; courage, a heart, a brain, an insight, a tool, a new lens with which to see life or experience ourselves; something that gives us the capacity to do what we have never done before, or never thought possible. We receive these gifts from the inner wisdom which hides behind the curtain only when we are ready to see it and receive it. These moments alert us, then, of our readiness to accept and take responsibility for our own strength, our own power, and our own capacity to heal ourselves. It means that we are ready to take our bliss seriously and risk the possibility that we deserve to live our fullest lives possible.

We are at the center of our own stories. This is not a form of egotism. It is a necessary recognition that *we are where the deep myths live out their stories.* They cannot live through us in full consciousness if we are not fully conscious. Our individual stories are of the utmost importance to the collective mythological stories of the human race. We need to know how to pay attention to the myths and the symbols we discover within ourselves, for when we connect with our souls and follow our bliss, we become the best gifts we can possibly be to the world. We also become better at receiving the gifts that others have to offer, celebrating them, and encouraging each other to nurture them.

We are the vehicles, both for our own individual myths and the great archetypal myths that we all share as a species. We need to learn how to show up at the crossroads of fate and destiny and balance the tension between the life we are living, and the life that is living us. We are simultaneously falling apart and putting ourselves back together again and again in an endless dance of creativity and destruction, death, and rebirth, will and surrender, love and loss, grief and joy. These are the truths that Dorothy discovers on her journey into and out of Oz. Embracing these truths and these characters within herself is what gives her strength and power, nurtured by her own growing wisdom and compassion. Now that Dorothy is aware of these many important parts of herself, she is responsible for keeping them alive and healthy, acknowledging and balancing the competing needs of each of them.

The thing we must understand about life is that it is, indeed, risky business. It is wild and untamed in so many ways. One of the few essential truths of existence is that nothing is permanent and there are no ultimate guarantees. Even if we choose to live under the illusion that we can escape life risk-free, it is nothing more than an illusion. For if we choose to live a so-called risk-free life, we are still taking a risk in not living our lives at all. Perhaps refusing to take any risks is the biggest risk of all. There is no way to not experience risk.

Because risk is such a fundamental part of life, it means that we are capable of being hurt, and when we do get hurt, we form resistances as a way of defending ourselves from getting hurt again. Therefore, resistance is also a fundamental part of life, the experience of which can also help us to initiate the journeys we must take to rediscover and reclaim our own wholeness. We must learn to honor our resistances before we can be successful at confronting them.

It can become quite easy to remain fixated on a particular resistance and remain stuck there. A resistance, like so many things, is not a place to stay forever, but merely a passage that we must learn to traverse. Even if we feel despair, exhaustion, and hopelessness in our ability to move through a resistance, the pressure to keep at it does not back off. It is here that it is good for us to remember yet again, that difficulty is not pathology, nor is it impossibility, even if it may appear that way to us at first. We have these inner wisdom characters that help us through it when the time comes and when we are ready to see and accept them.

When we become possessed by a resistance, we begin using words like "never" and "always." Phrases such as "I could *never* do that," or "I will *always* screw that up," are expressions I often hear from clients I work with that alert me to the presence of a strong resistance. When we succumb to our fears, we tend to gravitate toward those extreme polarities such as "always" and "never." In many ways, this reinforces the power of the resistance, but it plays a little sleight of hand in convincing us that because these things appear to be impossible that we no longer should take responsibility for them. Words like "always" and "never" protect us from having to take responsibility and engage in the possibility that we may have underestimated what we believed we were actually capable of. It is easier to believe the limits that our resistances try to reinforce than to have to take responsibility for the difficult tasks of moving through them and discovering the fullness of who we actually are.

It is the things we have determined to be impossible that hold the keys to what we most desperately need in life. I think it is safe to say that if one has determined something to be impossible in one's mind, then that is the first place that most needs to be explored for a resistance to be overcome. Further, our resistances will not let us try to sneak around these seemingly impossible places. They hold our feet to the fire until we finally agree to greet them and move through them. When we do this, we might have to admit (perhaps begrudgingly at first) that the very thing we determined to be impossible, is not only possible, but the necessary conundrum we needed to face in order to keep growing.

Chapter 10
Shame: The Tarasque

It is through learning how to accept and cherish who we already are that we give ourselves the opportunity to grow and change, not in searching to acquire that which we are not, and have convinced ourselves we need to be whole, happy and loved. This is a powerful paradoxical tension that we must learn to master throughout our lives. It reveals to us a core truth about the inherent wholeness and worthiness of being human. Shame, however, works tirelessly to convince us otherwise. Shame is a core belief that we are bad, ugly, insufficient, inept, corrupt with sin, etc. It runs very deep. There is a difference, however, between shame and guilt, which is an important distinction to make as we often confuse the two. If we notice ourselves feeling bad about treating ourselves or others poorly or unjustly, it is because we are feeling an appropriate emotion we have come to know as *guilt*. Guilt is the experience of knowing one has done wrong or made a careless mistake, recognizing the need to make amends for it. Guilt tells me that, "I messed up." Shame wants to tell me that I *am* "messed up." One is designed to address choices and behaviors while the other is an indictment of the core of one's own nature.

When someone who is suffering from deep, ongoing shame makes a mistake, their shame has them convinced that they couldn't have done it right even if they had tried. They made a mistake because they are inherently deficient somewhere inside. Shame is a very hideous and poisonous belief that often takes root very early in people's lives, depending on what kind of environment they were raised in. One does not heal oneself of shame by "being better," or working as hard as they can to be anyone other than who they are. One is healed by shame by first learning how to love oneself as one is. It is a difficult task, but not an impossible one, and it is helpful to remember that much of what we have determined in our own heads to be impossible for us to do is usually reflective of a narrative about ourselves being promoted by our own shame.

When I was in graduate school, I was taking a class where we did a little experiment to better understand the concept of shame and how it works from a more experiential perspective. The class organized their seats to form a giant circle around the room. We were then asked to anonymously write on a small piece of paper a memory that had caused us to experience a feeling of shame at some point in our lives. We were also asked to write on a separate piece of paper, a memory that we experienced of something affirming or healing in some way. We were then asked to pass our anonymous pieces of paper around the room so that everyone had somebody else's piece of paper.

To this day, I do not remember if I volunteered or was chosen to be the person who sat on a chair in the middle of the room surrounded in the circle by all my classmates and my professor. Fortunately, my only job was to sit in that chair. The professor randomly chose six people to read the piece of paper they had been given which shared a memory of an experience that provoked shame. For each piece of paper read out loud, a blanket was draped over my head. There were six blankets total. When we were done sharing memories of shame, six more people were chosen at random to read the healing affirmations written on the small pieces of paper. Each time an affirmation was read out loud, a blanket would be removed until I had no more blankets covering me.

After the exercise, I was asked to describe my entire experience throughout its duration. I noted how stuffy and confining it felt to be underneath all the blankets at once. This, of course, was meant to replicate the experience of shame. It feels stuffy and oppressive. It closes you off from the rest of the world. This experience was not all that surprising to me. The thing that did catch my attention, however, was the experience I had when the final blanket was removed. Even though I felt a sense of relief, accompanied by an increased ability to breathe more deeply and move around more freely, I also experienced a brief moment of feeling very exposed and frightened, wanting to hide back underneath the covers again.

In that moment, I understood that while the shame made me feel oppressed and confined, it also mimicked the feeling of a safe cocoon; an ability to hide and not be noticed. It was at this moment that the resistance around getting rid of shame for many people made more sense to me. I understood that while being completely destructive, shame is attempting, in its own way, to protect us from the possibility of getting hurt again, or at least, that is the illusion it conveys. It protects us from getting hurt by others by beating them to the punch. If we can tell ourselves how inadequate, horrible, or unlovable we are, then no one else has the opportunity to do it first. We stay "protected" from the judgments of others, but only at the expense of judging ourselves harshly, and harming ourselves even further. This, our shame imagines, softens the blow of

107

any harsh critique of our performance or judge of character from others. If someone is overly critical or wants to harm us outright, our shame tries to make sense of this by convincing us that somehow, *we must deserve it*. Somehow, we imagine, believing this softens the blow.

Shame prevents us from accepting ourselves just as we are. Shame convinces us that brokenness is our true nature, rather than a feeling we occasionally experience that provides us with an opportunity to grow beyond our current sense of inner fragmentation. It puts us in the double bind of consistently needing to be better while simultaneously convincing us that we cannot. We are in a constant state of spinning our wheels, trying to catch up and keep our heads above water, and ultimately working very hard to just survive. Left unattended for too long, shame can, and often does, become deadly. It keeps us drowning in pools that forbid us, not only to grow, but to experience any form of positive self-regard or self-love. Shame can also keep us in a perpetual state of anxiety.

Shame can take so many forms and likenesses. It is a clever chameleon. It moves into the confining corners and crevices of our mind and soul and conforms to whatever images we most fear or are most repulsed by and takes their shape. Once shame finds these spots it works very hard to convince us that these parts of us are the only ones that are real and true, and further, that they are irredeemable. Shame will exaggerate and distort these parts to gain more power over us.

A dragon of French legend, known as the *Tarasque*, is a creature that helps us to understand the nature of shame a little better. The Tarasque is described as a "nightmarish mix of animals." It carried on its body, "the head of a lion, a sturdy body protected by a turtle's shell, with a lashing, scaly tail tipped with a venomous sting, like a scorpion. It had six short, bear-like legs and was a vicious predator and famous menace to all of the people of southern France."[xx]

As a representation of shame itself, this particular mix of animals is interesting. The fierce head of the lion vigorously and perhaps even violently defends itself. The turtle shell is a protective mechanism, as shame attempts to protect us by shielding us from the unkind judgments of others. The scorpion tail represents the poisonous injection of our own harsh self-judgments before we allow anyone else to make them. It is also the poison we use to lash out against others that may choose to try and harm us with their own cruelty by giving them back a dose of our own "medicine," that is to say, our own sense of shame.

In one of the tales of the Tarasque, a salvific figure comes along to free a town that has been besieged by its oppression. A selfless sojourner by the name of St. Martha is summoned by the townspeople to slay the beast and free the town from its terror. St. Martha bravely ventures into the nearby wood where the Tarasque is rumored to retreat with its latest victim from the village to feed on. Indeed, St. Martha discovers the dragon in the act of feasting upon yet another villager. The Tarasque turns to confront St. Martha, who has lifted up two tree branches in the shape of a cross, a ward to prevent it from attacking her as she approaches it. Instantly, the dragon becomes tamed by the holy sight of St. Martha's makeshift crucifix. St. Martha sprinkles holy water over the dragon and fashions a collar made of braids from her own hair to lead the beast peacefully back to the village so it can make amends with the villagers and forge a truce.

The response of the townspeople, however, once they see the now docile beast being brought back to them, is predictably, a violent one. Too much carnage has occurred at its jaws. Too many friends and family have been lost to it. Once the people overcome their shock and awe at what St. Martha has accomplished, their anger and thirst for revenge overcomes them. As a mob, they attack the Tarasque, who is now no longer in any position to defend itself. Despite St. Martha's pleas for them to forgive the beast, the people of the town leave the great dragon dead.

One of the traps we need to be aware of, when confronting our own shame, is that as we begin to heal from it, we are likely to feel a swell of anger for having punished ourselves with shame in the first place, holding onto it for as long as we have. This is a tricky moment, for our anger may feel well justified, but if we act on this anger, we end up harming ourselves further as we punish ourselves with more shame. We need to look for a way to stop shaming ourselves for our own shame and learn to regard even it as a passing experience we all have from time to time. Using a mindfulness meditation, we can simply learn to acknowledge a sense of shame without fighting it, and then simply allow it to pass without having to attach ourselves to it. By doing so, we are not drawn into its drama, and we are less likely to be charmed by its tricks.

Shame is a very clever trickster. It will make use of any tools at its disposal, including tools of personal or religious piety, immediately chastising efforts to love ourselves by confusing self-love with arrogance of selfishness. It will try to scold us for feeling too proud of our accomplishments, accuse us of getting "a big head." How many of us confuse well-deserved pride of accomplishment with arrogance? How many of us have been told (or even whispered to ourselves) when celebrating a personal victory not to "toot our own horn?" Even humility gets confused with shame on a regular basis. The word itself brings up automatic feelings of shame, especially when the word takes on the form of *humiliation*.

There is nothing sacred that shame will not make use of to achieve its ends. It is parasitic in this way, only able to sustain life by latching on to whatever power we give it. The prospect of ridding oneself of shame, nevertheless, can feel so terrifying that one is not sure it is a survivable event, especially if it is all we've known and the only story we've ever been able to tell about ourselves. There is this underlying feeling that if one rids themselves of shame, then then they will die. More accurately, it is the story that our shame has promoted about us that needs to die. This is the double bind people feel when faced with the prospect of being healed from shame. So, when we finally wake up to what this dragon of shame has been doing to us, it is time to bring out the torches and the pitchforks! Shame is a dragon that must be slain! Right?

Not so fast. For when we play the game of dragon-slayer, we are playing shame's game. Just as we cannot heal judgment with more judgment, we cannot heal shame with more shame. When we can finally see our shame for what it is, our first response is likely to be one of deep anger and resentment, accompanied by a strong desire for retributive justice. All the other parts of our personality have been beaten down and held hostage by our shame, just like the villagers to whom St. Martha appeared. Our thirst for justice is very strong, and if we are not careful, will overpower our efforts to bring healing through the inner reconciliation process needed to really heal ourselves from our own feelings of shame.

As a therapist, I have become very familiar with the different ways that people experience and express shame. For some folks, shame has been a pervasive way of life, and they have never known anything else. For this reason, I have learned not to challenge someone's own shame right away. They are defending the only ego-ideal they have ever known, and if I am not able to hear and accept them in that place, at least at first, the message they will receive is that they are not to be taken seriously. I become one more person in their lives that refuses to see them and accept them as they are. I become yet another person that tells them they are wrong and incapable of getting it right. It is tricky business to side with someone's shame in order to help them learn to eventually let go of it. This shame has been serving them, however destructively, and that must be honored before it can be challenged.

Feelings, not just of an absence of self-worth, but also helplessness, are common to experiences of deep shame. So is the pervasive anxiety, that we must keep our true nature hidden from all others, in case they happen to find out just how worthless we believe ourselves to be. As we begin to learn how to heal ourselves from shame, we also need to be learning self-compassion along the way, and this includes compassion for our own shame. If we cannot cultivate compassion for our own shame, we will continue to punish ourselves every time we feel it. The more we punish our dragons, the more powerful they become, and the more connected we are to them, and this is no less true of our experiences of shame.

We each have a Tarasque, an inner wisdom figure like St. Martha, and an inner towns-worth of people that have felt imprisoned and brutalized by the Tarasque we carry inside of us. Understanding how the drama is set to play out is what allows us to know how to choreograph the most healing response to bring the resolution we are looking for from our suffering. The Tarasque must be brought into the light of day after it has been subdued so that we can fully look at what has been causing us so much trouble in the shadows. The braids of St. Martha's hair, fashioned into a collar and used to guide the Tarasque back into town, is a powerful symbol for the promise of healing and reconciliation. The shame is being tethered, but by something that is meant to bring reconciliation rather than retribution. It symbolizes the hope that our shame can be subdued, and that we can once again learn to cultivate peace within our hearts with the freedom to grow and learn again.

When we greet even our own shame with curiosity, the curiosity disarms it. It no longer has any control over us. We learn very quickly that it has no power to keep us imprisoned and that it never really did. Like all our dragons, shame is only as powerful as we allow it to be. We are free to feel whatever it is we need to feel without apology, even moments when we experience our own shame. This is what prevents us from getting stuck to the story of our own shame. We accept rather than fight all of the different feelings we experience. Beneath the wounds that our shame has been hiding from us, we finally gain access to the tender and vulnerable parts of ourselves that have been neglected and abandoned. We now stand a chance to get to know these more tender parts of ourselves and allow them to share their gifts with us.

We no longer must be afraid of these parts of ourselves because we learn that what we experience so often as a weakness, indeed has its own quiet strength and wisdom. Fleeting moments and shadows of shame may always come to visit us throughout our lives, but if we have discovered healing, we know how to utilize those moments as invitations to pay attention to the soul, rather than confuse ourselves with our own shame, or let it destroy the soul. In this sense, these moments simply become nothing more and nothing less than information designed to alert us that something is feeling neglected within us that needs our attention and care. One way we know that we are successfully healing ourselves of shame is when we begin to experience true gratitude again, or in some cases, for the very first time. Once we begin to deal with our shame appropriately, it becomes more realistic for us to confront our fears and be honest with ourselves about them.

Chapter 11
Fear: The Sister Dragon of Childe Wynde

Fear is one of the most powerful, intoxicating and paralyzing feelings we can experience. Depending on how powerful the fear is, we can become easily possessed and controlled by it. We forget, in these moments when we experience fear, that the only power it has over us is our willingness to do what it tells us to do. Unrecognized and undealt-with fear turns into a dangerous projection onto others. The fear we have regarding our rejected shadows, often turns into forms of violence and hatred toward those we have projected that fear onto. Fear can convince us to abandon our own reason and logic and act out in bizarre ways. It can, if it's powerful enough, convince us that a friend is an enemy and that the truth is a lie. Fear, untended to, can possess and control us, almost as if it is using our mind and body to believe and do things we would not normally believe and do.

Fear does serve a purpose that is fundamental to our survival. It is an emotional and physiological response to a threat or a perceived threat. Fear is designed to keep us safe and alive by alerting us of the need to protect ourselves. Fear is also helpful in teaching us how to pay attention and not take things for granted when we are learning to do something new. It can keep our senses sharp. It can also signal to us that an important shift in our lives may be approaching. Our status quo feels threatened and produces the experience of fear. Fear can be useful in many situations and in small doses. Prolonged fear, however, can overcome our lives and swallow up all the many parts of our psyche that are valued and needed by us. It is important to learn how to greet fear and manage it well.

Fear, unrecognized and untended to, can quickly become a powerful and frightening dragon, as we shall see in the following tale. The story of Childe Wynde and his dragon sister is an English legend, most likely of Welsh origin. Childe Wynde is the son of a king who is off to war, his presence a noticeable absence from the kingdom. Left behind is his father, the King, and his princess sister, Margaret. Their mother, the Queen, has long since passed away, and the

King has recently (and secretly) become engaged to a new suitor. This soon-to-be Queen, however, is mysterious and aloof, seldom showing her presence at any social functions, and not well-known by either Margaret or Childe. Nevertheless, the King is married to her.

Rumors begin to circle that there is something suspicious about this new Queen, and accusations of her cruelty begin to surface among the people. The only one who seems aloof to this is the King himself, behaving almost as though an enchantment has been placed upon him. On the night of their wedding, she gets the King drunk and makes sure he is passed out late into the evening.

Stealing away to a solitary place, this new Queen begins to perform some magic. Beneath the moonlight, she begins to weave a tapestry of fine silver thread in the form of the sleeping princess Margaret. When Margaret awakes in the morning, she discovers that she is suffering from a great pain and agony. She begins to flail her body around and, much to her own alarm, finds herself destroying most of the contents of her bedroom in ways that should not have been humanly possible for her to do.

She takes a look at her hands and notices that they are claws. She sees an image of herself in her mirror and discovers a dragon looking back at her. When she cries out in agony, she notices that her voice is that of the giant roar of a monster. Horrified, she fights her way out of her room in the castle and flies off into the wilderness.

Margaret begins to experience the hunger of a dragon, and almost against her own will, finds herself feasting on the livestock of the farmers residing in the kingdom, filled with an insatiable hunger. She weeps in agony for what she has done and for what she knows she will continue to do in wreaking havoc on the animals and the people of the countryside. She has to keep moving from one place to the next as she is attacked by men and guards of the kingdom in a vain effort to protect themselves and their property from her destructive hunger.

The King, during all of this, continues to remain aloof, until an old man, who has perceived the truth of the dark magic at work, encourages the King to call his son home from the war to face the dragon. The King does so willingly. The old man also encourages the King to banish or murder his wife, as he identifies the new Queen as the perpetrator of this dark magic. Strangely, the King ignores this advice and instead, imprisons the new Queen in a lonely tower of the castle.

Childe Wynde, having received the news from his father and the summons to come home, first fashions his ship with wood from a pear tree, long believed to be a material resistant to magical curses and dark sorcery. As predicted, the new Queen, still able to perform her magic while imprisoned, sets a swarm of sea furies against Childe Wynde's ship in order to sink it. The wood, however, proves strong enough to stave off this onslaught.

The new Queen is now forced to up the ante, and she does this by taking possession of the sister dragon, Margaret, and uses her to attack Childe Wynde's ship before it can reach the shore of the kingdom. This she does successfully, and Childe Wynde finds himself having to swim back to shore.

When he reaches the shore, the smoke from the carnage of the day still lies heavily about him, and he begins to notice the glowing eyes of the dragon that is his sister Margaret, bearing down on him. The dragon is getting ready to eat him, when it pauses. The will of Margaret has just enough power to stay the will of the new Queen for an extra moment to whisper a message to her brother. She tells him that he must kiss her three times in order to break the spell upon Margaret and remove her curse. She warns him, however, that this will be dangerous for him to do. So sharp and rough are her scales that even a simple kiss will pierce his flesh.

Childe Wynde does as he is instructed, however, each time he gives the dragon a kiss, its spines pierce his flesh a little deeper, the last actually piercing through his cheek entirely. Wounded, and in pain, Childe Wynde is nevertheless successful. The shape of the dragon shrivels and falls dead to the ground. The guards rush to uncover what they hope will be the body of the princess Margaret, finding her weak and in pain, but alive.

The King is overjoyed to have his daughter returned to him, and for the ordeal of her dragon-hood to be over with. Childe Wynde requests his father to have the new Queen put to death, but the King still refuses to do this. Childe Wynde then decides to make a bargain with his father that he will merely bring to the new Queen a piece of the broken ship made of pear wood and touch her with it. Childe Wynde suspects that this new Queen is in fact, a witch, and the properties of the pear wood will reveal whether or not this is true. The king agrees to this. Childe Wynde approaches a cowering Queen, trapped in her tower prison with the pear wood. Upon touching the queen with the pear wood, she is instantly transformed back into a toad, revealed to be her true form.

There is a lot of imagery to unpack from this tale. One of the first things we must acknowledge is how hard many of these European myths are on witches and stepmothers. They are routinely symbols of evil, dark magic, and cruelty. Even though, there is a redemptive element of the Divine Feminine in the form of the princess Margaret and the long-passed Queen Mother, the idea that it is the dark feminine powers and wiles that are dangerous and corrupting to men and Kings, is routinely promoted in many of these fairy tales. In spite of this bias, the symbolism of the characters remains powerful, and the tasks of recognizing how our fears work through the lessons of the story remain the same for all of us, women and men alike.

To read this story mythologically, we must understand the role of each figure as it belongs to the King, who is routinely a symbol of the Self, or Soul, when it comes to Western myths. In this sense, the King is responsible for each and every character in the story itself, each a representation of a different part of his own psyche. The King's slumbering Divine Feminine presence has been torn in two. The witch and the daughter represent two different aspects of the rejected Divine Feminine presence in the King's life. The King is unconscious of both of them. Left to themselves, they are at war with each other, one of them trying to keep the King unconscious, the other trying to wake him up.

The King, like the Half-Man, lost his original connection to the Divine Feminine when his wife and mother of his children passed away. He has not done his grief work, and as a result, has allowed himself to become "bewitched" by the wish-fulfillment of a magical mother of sorts; someone who can protect him from all experiences of pain or harm. It accomplishes this by inebriating him, by making him *numb* to his own brokenness. This, in turn, actually prevents him from recognizing his need to do his own work, reviving the Divine Feminine within him and taking responsibility for it. His daughter, whose plight he has ignored, provokes the wrath of the witch to turn her into a dragon.

The more the king fails to recognize his inner, Divine Feminine, the more dragon-like it becomes to get his attention. In this way, the daughter and the witch become unwitting collaborators to wake him up. Their escalated antagonism toward each other serves this purpose, alerting the King of his need to resolve his own brokenness. He needs the help, however, of the Divine Masculine energy, in the form of his son, to instigate the drama to unfold in just the right way, ensuring that the King will not be able to ignore his daughter, the dragon. His son is young enough to remember the importance of the healed and reintegrated Divine Feminine, and so his son is bearing the wounded Divine Masculine part of the King who had forgotten about the importance of the divine union of the Syzygy. They instigate the necessary confrontation that must take place, and both of their lives must become threatened in a pronounced way for the King to finally wake up and remember what his true work is.

The King continues to resist the task of killing the witch. It is important that we regard the act of murder in this sense, not literally, but symbolically. The act of killing in the psyche, has more to do with inner transformation. What the King must kill is his need to remain numb and unconscious to his own wounded and fragmented Divine Feminine. When he is able to kill off this need, or this ego-ideal, he is then able to take responsibility for cultivating the Divine Feminine within himself. As we saw in the stories of Vasalisa and Ivan, when the principle is internalized, it ceases to be an outer figure, whether that figure is a wisdom guide or an antagonist. The witch turns back into a toad and the dragon turns back into his daughter.

What has been ruling our King this entire time has been fear, and for the most part, the King has been unconscious of it. He only really becomes aware of his own fear when he is left with no other option but to risk the death of his new Queen, the witch. Be it a witch or a sorcerer, the magical principle is important imagery to invoke here, because fear is something that keeps us under its spell. The witch could not tolerate the presence of the Divine Feminine alive within the King himself, in the form of his daughter, the princess. In order to remove this threat, she needed to transform the princess into a blood-thirsty dragon.

Interestingly enough, the only way that the curse of the fear can initially be broken, is by the actions of the prince, Childe Wynde. It is his task to enact the courage that the King, in his stupor, has abandoned. He must face the strong possibility that he will die when he faces his sister-dragon, knowing that she has been bewitched by the new Queen and is being controlled by her. His instinct is, as it is for us as well, the fight or flight response. His ability to hear the voice of his sister inside the dragon and follow her instructions is an act of pure courage and bravery, for he is still not safe. He knows what he is risking by kissing the dragon three times. He knows that even this action is going to hurt. The prince's courage here, one of both strength and self-sacrifice, is a vision of what a healthy and integrated Divine Masculine energy is intended to be. The Divine Masculine knows when to fight and when to surrender, putting the needs of the whole above his own when called for, and understanding that he belongs to the whole, and the whole belongs to him. The prince knows that his love for his sister, and his deep love for his people, may put him in harm's way. He may have to be willing to get hurt.

This is exactly what it feels like when we confront our own deep fears. It hurts. Perhaps we not only have to face the fear itself, but we must also make ourselves aware of things that we have done while being possessed by our own fears. Facing fear is an ego-crippling experience. We see just how difficult it is for the King, right up to the very end, to acknowledge the full reality of his own fear and the depth of his own brokenness. The King cannot come to this place on his own. He needs the power and wisdom of all of his inner characters, working together to bring him to the full realization of what he has done to himself. He needs the deep soul wisdom of the "old man" to instigate his journey, and he needs the reunion of the Divine Feminine and Masculine, symbolized by his daughter and son, working together again to give him the strength to do what must be done. He needed the presence of the witch to instigate the right struggle at the right time for him.

How Childe Wynde faces this dragon is important, because the conventional wisdom of dragon-slaying will not work here. He is instructed to kiss the dragon even though this will harm him, in order to break the spell. Again, the death of the dragon in this story symbolizes a transformation taking place. Now, that the Divine Feminine has been recognized again, it no longer has to clothe itself in the form of an antagonistic dragon. It is now free to do its job, and as we learn, it still has more work to do to rescue the King from his own stupor, still tolerating the presence of the witch, and his failure to let go of the magical principle which removes him from his own responsibility to face his fear and instigate his own healing.

The presence of fear in our lives underscores the importance of nurturing the inner, collective community of the psyche. Without it, we are lost and possessed by fear, greed, power, self-loathing and other such things. Without it, we are at the mercy of a belief that magic tricks can be performed, not to help heal the brokenness within us, but to give us the illusion of peace by becoming numb to our own pain and fear. We invoke the magical principle when we are afraid, because we feel helpless. Rather than cultivate tenderness and compassion for ourselves in these places, we often retreat into a form of unconsciousness in an effort to cover it up and numb it out.

We must also recognize the pressures being applied by our modern culture, which promotes the idea that expressing fear is a sign of weakness. One of the reasons why we avoid dealing with our own fears is because we value the *appearance* of self-assurance and self-confidence. This can actually serve a valuable social function for us for a while, as we attempt to continue managing day-to-day life. The problem with this is that we are acting out of our own half-ness when we do this for too long. Genuine self-assurance and confidence are nothing more and nothing less than an ability to know who we are, like who are and not have to apologize to other people for who we are. Nowhere in that definition are we being asked to deny all of the different emotions we are likely to feel, including fear. Self-confidence is not about projecting an image of strength that is somehow unmoved by fear. In fact, that is the opposite of self-confidence. Self-confidence includes our ability to practice courage, humility, compassion, and bravery. None of these things can be exercised without the experience of fear, and often one of the most courageous things we can ever do is recognize our most vulnerable emotions as being valid and worthy of our care and compassion.

Recognizing and greeting our own fears does not only bring inner healing and reconciliation for ourselves. It allows us to practice these virtues with others. We stop projecting our fears onto others, which serves to dehumanize them, and we begin to see the image of divine wholeness imprinted on all people, even the ones we do not like. Love, compassion and humility are the antidotes to fear, along with our ability to remain curious about ourselves and others.

Chapter 12
Anger: Grendel, Cain and Hyde

Anger can be a great ally when it is consciously embraced and utilized to its purpose. The experience of anger is the natural response to a violation of one's safety, respect, and personal values. Anger can be a useful tool to speak up for ourselves and for others when we feel like we are being violated. Anger often becomes the voice for more vulnerable feelings such as sadness, fear and embarrassment, protecting those feelings in the face of others who do not deserve to have access to them. Anger can motivate us to act when we may have been complacent and help us summon the courage to do so. Anger can also easily become one of the most threatening and destructive dragons we can ever contend with if it is acting unconsciously and brutally. Anger, untended, can quickly turn into malice. Malice turns into violence.

Anger is both, enslaver and emancipator, ally and dragon. There is no other emotion that illuminates so clearly the need to balance immense paradoxical tensions such as anger. There is also no other emotion that can possess us so completely if we let it. Our relationship with our anger is important. With it, we can create and destroy. Knowing how much anger is necessary and enough and discerning when anger becomes counter-productive, destructive or oppressive can constitute a very thin line. Of all our dragons, anger can be one of the most difficult and important for us to tame.

If we take the time to explore our own shadows, we may begin to discover where our anger was born, what feeds it and where it is likely to get triggered within us. Anger is both internalized and externalized energy. It can act out (and act in) with brutality. Internalized brutality can be just as destructive as outward brutality, and is less likely to be noticed by others, which can make it even more dangerous to individuals brutalizing themselves with it. Keeping our anger hidden may seem like a better alternative in the moment than letting it erupt onto others around us, which may be true to a certain extent. If we do not, however, learn to acknowledge, honor, and heal our own anger, we will not only destroy ourselves, but we are likely to, at some point, have a strong outward burst of it that overrides our ability to control it inwardly. In other words, bottled up anger eventually explodes.

Accessing our own anger appears threatening to us unconsciously as well, because to do so we may have to feel whatever vulnerable emotions are lying beneath that anger. If we have not done our own grief work with sadness and fear, we may find it intolerable to allow ourselves to feel those things again, particularly if we have been traumatized, felt taken advantage of or abused in the past when some of those vulnerable feelings may have been exposed to others who used them to hurt us. Much like shame, the dragon of anger is attempting to protect us from ever getting hurt again. If anyone tries to threaten the safety of that, the dragon will lash out, with a vengeance if need be, to protect one from that possibility.

So, in addition to using anger to practice courage and fortitude, our anger can also become part of our matrix of defense mechanisms to protect us from any threats, real or imagined. Our relationship with our own anger can be very complex, and this fact alone can make us feel intimidated by it, particularly because it is so powerful. It takes no lack of courage for us to learn to greet our own anger with compassion and mindfulness. For most of us, life leaves us little choice but to learn how to cultivate that courage because anger is a necessary part of human life.

Unexamined and unresolved anger become projections quickly and fortify defensiveness. One way we avoid our shadows is to lash out at them in anger, attacking any dragon that attempts to show us an unresolved fear, wound or insecurity for us to mend. These dragons are intolerable to us, but the energy of the dragon is still there. We go looking for ways to expel that energy, and there is no quicker way of expelling it than projecting it onto someone else. If we have little control over our own anger, we are also in danger of acting on that projection and harming the person who carries it for us.

The story of unexamined anger that leads to projection has been with us from the very beginning. In the book of Genesis, of the Hebrew Bible, Cain and Abel are known as the children of Adam and Eve, the mythic first inhabitants of the Earth. Cain, in his jealousy of his brother, murders him. His unresolved anger lashes out and he becomes possessed by it. This act of violence is the consequence of a world where sin has been allowed to prevail. Fear, anger, greed and jealousy have been allowed to enter into the human imagination, and therefore the human experience. Cain is the first "bad guy," succumbed to his evil impulses, ensuring that this same evil will continue to be propagated throughout his lineage. It is Cain's lineage that reappears in the myth of Beowulf.

In the epic poem *Beowulf*, the Grendel creature is the mythological embodiment of the corrupted line of creatures that traces its lineage back to Cain. Cain represents the first mythic symbol of one who has become possessed by his shadow. Grendel is the continued embodiment of all that is evil, corrupt and vile. Grendel is the embodiment of a feral form of anger geared toward violence and destruction. He is a creature driven by pure rage and lust for destruction. In the halls of Hrothgar, where deeds of courage are shared, and merriment abounds, lives nevertheless, a most terrifying beast.

> *"A powerful monster, living down*
> *In the darkness, growled in pain, impatient*
> *As day after day the music rang*
> *Loud in that hall, the harp's rejoicing*
> *Call and the poet's clear songs, sung*
> *Of the ancient beginnings of us all"*[xxi]

Grendel's thick skin cannot be pierced by any sword or arrow. The women and men of Hrothgar's halls are at Grendel's complete mercy, as one by one he comes in the night to kidnap, slaughter, and feast on them. Grendel, a creature thoroughly corrupted by sin and evil, is incapable of being redeemed by God, "whose love Grendel could not know." He has no virtue to speak of, not even that which is hidden. Conversely, the hero of the story, Beowulf, has no shadow-side to speak of. Even his pride and desperate need for fame and glory never manifest as an aspect of his own unexamined shadow, or as any kind of character flaw. Rather, it is endlessly glorified throughout the story. The story of Beowulf and Grendel is the continuing story of the Western Psyche, forever at war with itself. The greater the need for a sinless, untarnished hero, the greater the evil that must present itself as the hero's antithesis.

If Grendel is, in fact, Beowulf's rejected shadow (which I believe to be a psychologically honest interpretation of the poem), it can tell us something about just how powerful the opposites can be when we give up balancing the tension between the two and become possessed by the need to pit one against the other. Beowulf's desperate need to appear strong and virtuous, forsaking all other virtues for the virtue of fame and glory, and to be worshipped for it, finds an equally strong antithesis in the Grendel character. *The more completely we reject the shadow parts of ourselves, the more completely monstrous, menacing and evil they become.* Beowulf needs an embodiment of pure evil to counterbalance his pure virtue. The more virtuous Beowulf needs to be, the more thoroughly evil his shadow side must become.

Even at the end of his life, when Beowulf faces a proper dragon, he does not risk any crack in the façade of the untarnished and apotheosized strength and virtue he has built his entire persona, and hence life, around. He would rather the dragon consume him in a glorious death, than attempt to surrender his ego-ideal as a single-minded warrior. Beowulf has no capacity to entertain such an idea in his imagination. He is too consumed by his need for glory to surrender his ego to his shadow, and predictably, his dragon defeats him.

Beowulf's rigid arrogance, resulting in his inevitable death, represents a stage where I believe we find ourselves stuck in our Western development, even as some important paradigm shifts are pressing down on us. The changes we must make for the sake of our species' survival are only evil to the extent that we decide they must be. The ability to change, adapt, and be flexible is part of our inheritance as human beings who, like all living creatures, are programmed for survival. In addition to knowing when it is time to stand strong and resist, we must also know how to let go and make way. Since, we have not allowed the concept of surrender to be added our codex of Western virtues, we only know how to cling desperately to our ability to fight it out to the bitter end, ensuring our inability to be adaptable. Will we remain stubborn and go down fighting like Beowulf, or can we adjust, learn to greet our shadows and come to terms with the changes that life has in store for us?

What is interesting throughout the story is that the rage of the Grendel creature is matched only by the righteous indignation of Beowulf himself. Beowulf has characterized his rage as a righteous rage, blessed and ordained by God, while the rage of the Grendel is only characterized by his own deep hatred and lust for revenge. Even Grendel's mother, who nearly defeats Beowulf after taking revenge for the death of her son at his hands, is not given due justification for her anger. Both Beowulf and Grendel are irrevocably and unapologetically one-sided and one-dimensional. If Grendel is Beowulf's shadow side, he remains split and condemned to the furthest reaches of his unexamined shadow until the bitter end. Beowulf would rather end his life than have to come to terms with his own shadow, too overcome and overwhelmed by his own pride and greed for untarnished virtue. In this sense, Beowulf becomes a tragic character, victim of his own arrogance and inability to self-examine. He becomes a victim of his own dragons.

Jekyll and Hyde

Respectability and repression are the two central themes in tension with each other, in Robert Louis Stevenson's story set in the context of a highly Puritanical society nestled in the heart of nineteenth century London. It is through the excessive need for respectability accompanied by the obsessive personal piety of Dr. Jekyll, that he seeks to rid his conscience of his lower passions by splitting them off into a complete and wholly different personality. He brings Edward Hyde into existence, to entertain his shadow personality and give it the autonomy of a distinct individual, separate from Dr. Jekyll. He believes that this will free him from whatever temptations he imagines are holding him back from being admired completely, as an upstanding and respectable citizen. Jekyll imagines that by sequestering this dark part of himself off, that he is strengthening his virtuous nature even more. Dr. Jekyll recounts his fantasy. "If each, I told myself, could be housed in separate identities, life would be relieved of all that was unbearable; the unjust might go his way, delivered from the aspirations and remorse of his more upright twin."[xxii]

Jekyll is dealing with a much more subtle and subdued form of anger directed toward himself, causing an inner fragmentation to take root. His own darkness, and the intense corresponding shame, buckles under the pressures to conform to the pious expectations of his time. Thus, he begins his quest to sequester these undesirable traits within himself into a persona that can express itself without guilt or conscience. In a way, his quest is not unlike the search for the fountain of eternal youth, except that Jekyll's fountain is one of eternal *virtue*, unfettered by the more unsavory parts of his personality. Jekyll's daydream of living a life of total virtue without guilt or sin is powerful enough for him to experiment scientifically with how he might separate the two sides of himself into two completely, and wholly autonomous, personalities. Jekyll decides to invent an elixir that allows him to transform into Mr. Hyde whenever he wants.

At first, Henry Jekyll is the one who feels as though he is in complete control of this experiment. He becomes Hyde whenever *he* chooses to and does not bother to be too concerned about Hyde's exploits as long as the transgressions are not too heinous, allowing himself to cast off any feelings of guilt or responsibility for Hyde's behavior; almost looking upon them with some measure of amusement. It is not until Hyde's transgressions become deadly that Jekyll begins to fear Hyde. Eventually the doctor learns that Hyde has been plotting to take over executive function of Jekyll's personality. Jekyll soon learns that he needs the transformation potion, not to become Mr. Hyde any longer, but to remain Dr. Jekyll. Hyde begins acting like an addiction does, slowly taking over Jekyll's entire personality, and driving all his needs.

Stevenson is playing with the shadow principle in this short tale. Once again, we can draw the conclusion that neither repression of, nor possession by, the shadow gives us what we need to be whole, responsible human beings.

As a matter of fact, either one is likely to lead to disaster. Jekyll finally recognizes, too late, that he is responsible for his own shadow and his own evil. He begins to understand the terrifying consequences of his inability to tame his own dragons. In one of Jekyll's last written accounts as himself, he notes, "I have been made to learn that the doom and burden of our life is bound for ever on man's shoulders, and when the attempt is made to cast it off, it but returns upon us with more unfamiliar and more awful pressure."[xxiii]

Mr. Hyde is the result of Jekyll's attempt to cut off and quarantine the undesirable parts of his personality and cast them into his shadow rather than learn to acknowledge, tame and take responsibility for them. Eventually, Jekyll discovers that it is not he who is in control of Hyde, but rather the other way around. In rejecting his shadow, Jekyll gave it overwhelming power to consume him.

Dr. Jekyll's pride regarding his personal reputation as a respectable citizen was at stake. This was his ego-ideal, and it was very strong, so strong that he inadvertently created a shadow creature just as strong to match it. His own pride coupled with the pressures of a social standard he had worked hard to conform to, taught him to fear these shadow principles and cast them further into the utter darkness. Dr. Jekyll's curiosity is quickly silenced by his own fear and shame, unable to seek forgiveness and reconciliation. When we cut off our ability to reconcile ourselves with our own capacity for anger, greed, hate or other things that we fear about ourselves, we are only more likely to embody those principles in unconscious and destructive ways.

Mr. Hyde is a result of Dr. Jekyll's failure to acknowledge and embrace his own shadow. Stevenson's not-so-subtle jab at the Puritanical culture of his time is being put on trial as to its benefit to humankind and modern society, but so is the unexamined life. Clearly, this tale intends to show that Jekyll, a symbol for the social piety of the day, is failing miserably in his task to bring the balance and civility he has been striving for. Hyde is the dragon-like embodiment of all of Dr. Jekyll's unacknowledged shadows which come to possess him and then act out in malice.

Hyde, like Cain and Grendel, is the embodiment of pure evil. Hyde provided Dr. Jekyll with an excuse to act out his own darkness without having to take responsibility for it. When people are taught to do the same, and get too close to their own inner darkness, they immediately throw that darkness onto another person, another group, another political party, another religion, and in Jekyll's case, a split personality. Hyde is not just Jekyll's burden, however. It is the burden of all who choose to fight or flee the knowledge of their own shadows, projecting them endlessly into the world around them. The whole world is erupting in violence trying to destroy Mr. Hyde, not understanding that he exists not "out there," but in their own hearts and minds.

When we choose to hide (Hyde) our anger and do not give it a voice, it takes on a personality of its own and begins to act out in destructive ways. We ought to look with respect on the intense feeling of anger and what it can inspire us to do. It is powerful enough that it is one of the few emotions that are socially acceptable for Western men, in particular, to express, even in the context of a patriarchal culture that demands of our men an emotionally detached response toward life and toward themselves. Even then, anger is mostly dealt with in a very unconscious way, leading to destructive behaviors that only perpetuate further fragmentation from vulnerable emotions.

The more thoroughly we reject that anger, as with all elements of our own shadows, the more monstrous and possessive of us it becomes. Remember my little parabolic warning at the beginning of the book; when we treat some part of us as an enemy, we can expect it to behave as an enemy. Responding with wisdom, compassion and resolve will change the nature of the dragons that are causing us so many problems. When we have compassion toward our anger, it no longer must scream and yell at us to get our attention. We are free to both use it wisely and encourage it to step aside when it becomes too overwhelming or is not in our best interest.

The reconciliation between ourselves and our own capacity for anger is important as we journey into adulthood. It is what allows us to let the scales fall from our eyes when our innocence and naiveté will no longer suffice to keep us accountable to our journeys of our soul, and we begin to recognize that we are not living up to the fullness of who we are and what we are capable of becoming. It is what initiates the journey when we realize that the people we wanted to rely on to give us our happiness are not capable of it, and we must learn to take responsibility for our own happiness. When we wake up to just how precious and important we are, we can begin to experience anger about all the injustices we have been subjected to, whether by our own hand or by the hands of others. Our anger initially teaches us to stand up for our inherent dignity and self-worth. Our anger becomes a motivation to want to protect others from suffering injustice as well. If we do not resolve it however, that anger quickly turns into resentment, bitterness and hostility, both toward ourselves and others.

When we incorporate our anger meaningfully into our psyches, it is free to act as a source of motivation, energy and even wisdom. It is initially there to speak up for our worth, particularly if we feel it being threatened. Our anger can inspire us to change something about ourselves that we have felt unwilling or unable to change. Our anger can motivate us to stand up to all kinds of injustice we see around us. Our anger can teach us to speak truth in love, discover a kind of courage that has eluded us, and strengthen our resolve to enter the next challenge in our lives when we have been feeling too complacent. Our anger can rescue us from prolonged indecisiveness.

When we learn to acknowledge, accept, and meaningfully interact with our anger as an ally, it can become a very powerful one when we need it. The dragon of anger is one that we need to greet and feel, so it can be transformed into the ally we need it to be. If we do not, we run the real risk of that anger turning into something much more potentially harmful. Experiencing our anger, giving it a voice, and allowing it to speak when we need it to, is important to our overall health and well-being. As well, we need to be aware when we have been carrying around our anger longer than it is healthy for us to do so, so it does not become destructive toward others or corrosive toward us. Again, we must remember the importance of balancing tensions within us. The unexamined, unresolved, and projected anger becomes the even more dangerous dragon of war. It is to that we turn in the next chapter.

Chapter 13
War, Greed and Power: The Desolation of Smaug

Slaying a dragon does not solve one's problems nor does it bring peace. It produces the opposite result. Such an attitude toward dragons betrays an assumption that they should not exist in the first place. The presence, then, of a dragon becomes a necessary evil that must be removed or destroyed. It is an aberration. It does not belong to the proper order of things. Its very existence is a threat. Much of what provides the impetus for war and terror in our world, operates from an assumption that our lives should be free of all things, or people, that would cause us any trouble. We have created institutions dedicated to this principle of protecting the status quo at all costs. They arise as unhealthy forms of tribalism, religious fundamentalism, fascism, xenophobia, racism, classism, homophobia, etc., the components of which fuel all wars.

Earlier in the book, I talked about how an eternal feeling of security and safety are childhood fantasies. These are wish-fulfillments to stay connected to the womb and avoid our journeys into the unknown. Life has its own way of pushing us out of that womb as we grow up and become adults. We either learn to sacrifice our desire to protect the status quo and allow for the possibility of being changed by people we meet and events that happen to us, or we choose to fight it. Sometimes these encounters do present real threats and real evil, and it is important to know how to protect and even defend ourselves. Often, however, our need to protect ourselves is predicated on an assumption that any change is an indictment on our way of life, and therefore a threat to it. Living an abundant life, however, does not mean living a safe or uniform life where we are never asked to change, adjust or adapt. We cannot stay still or move backward. Life moves forward, with us or without us. Our ability to adapt is crucial to our own growth and well-being, not just as individual people, but as communities and nations.

Yet, what do we hear from politicians when our cultural myths and accustomed ways of life feel threatened? We hear them reassuring us that they can provide that sense of safety and security for us. Big promises are made to protect the status quo at all costs. How they will get it done is by making promises to stop all possibilities of harm coming our way, often (and ironically) by making promises to threaten harm toward others to achieve this end. Thus, we begin the process of identifying who is a potential threat or enemy to us. This is how war begins; often at the hands of special interests, greed and a jockeying for power. Our leaders play on the deepest fears of our hearts to garner our support. Again, this is not to say that there are no real threats in the world that we must defend ourselves from, but it does underscore the idea that war begins in the heart long before a battle ever takes place, or an act of terror is committed.

To completely abnegate all responsibility for war, and the threat it poses, onto our political leaders and demagogues would be disingenuous, however, for these leaders carry with them the projections of all our human fears and desires, including those parts that wish to wage war on our enemies. War ultimately begins in the unresolved conflicts of the human heart, which we eventually learn to project outward toward others. We are all complicit in, and responsible on some level for, our wars. To bring an end to war, one must come to terms with the reality of war inside one's own heart. To become possessed by or remain in denial of the war inside our own hearts is what ultimately leads to our unexamined shadows acting out in war, making use of the tools of brutality and violence to enact it.

In Greek mythology *Ares* (also known as Mars, in Roman mythology) is the god of war. Consistently hated by Zeus and often finding himself on the losing side of many battles with Zeus, he is accompanied into war by his companions *Deimos* (god of terror) and *Phobos* (god of fear). His conundrum is that the only real spoils of war are more of the same fear and insecurity, the likes of which those who wage war set out to eradicate in an effort to secure peace and prosperity. The spoils of war often end up bringing more curses upon those who reap them by perpetuating endless cycles of violence and retribution.

War is the culmination of many things working together, such as greed, hubris, pathological self-interest, jealousy, revenge and wrath. The dragon *Smaug* embodies all of these qualities. In J.R.R. Tolkien's classic tale of *The Hobbit*, a privileged and somewhat complacent hobbit by the name of Bilbo Baggins must come to terms with his destiny to confront a dragon sitting on a hoard of stolen treasure. Smaug is described as having a "wicked and wily heart." He is clever and knows how to bide his time, but his anger and hatred are easily provoked, and his pride easily offended. He is fiercely obsessed with only one thing: the treasure he has stolen from the dwarves of long ago. He will suffer no rival to his claim on even one piece of that treasure.

In the story, Bilbo's first encounter with Smaug occurs while the dragon is fast asleep. Bilbo manages to steal a valuable cup from the treasure hoard to bring back to his dwarf companions still resting outside of the long passageway leading into the heart of the Great Lonely Mountain, where Smaug has established his lair. When Smaug awakes, he is instantly aware of the theft. "Thieves! Fire! Murder! Such a thing had not happened since first he came to the Mountain! His rage passes description… His fire belched forth, the hall smoked, he shook the mountain-roots."[xxiv]

Eventually Smaug is driven from the mountain after a battle with the dwarves to reclaim their kingdom, taking off into the night air, filled with a consuming vengeance and lust for retribution and destruction. He decides to take out his anger on the small village of Laketown, residing on an island in the middle of a vast lake that sits close to the mountain. He brings fire, death, and ruin down upon the town and all its residents. Smaug represents our unconscious greed and hatred that brew deeply in the unexamined regions of our own shadows, and then erupt into war when they are provoked. These fiery passions make no distinction between the guilty and the innocent, bringing death and ruin to any and all who happen to be in their way.

The treasures we hoard and protect with alarming fervor do not simply have to be material goods and possessions. They can be thoughts, beliefs, prejudices, wounds, long-held resentments and social norms we have kept precious to us in some way. All of us have some form of treasure we are hoarding away and protecting from someone else who might threaten to take it from us. All of us have something that we are willing to go to war for.

Thorin, the dwarf lord whose birthright is to reclaim the Lonely Mountain and its treasure hoard, begins to mirror Smaug's qualities as he descends into a myopic greed of his own after reclaiming his mountain treasures again. The treasure itself has been cursed by the long sleep of Smaug and slowly drags Thorin into a possession of his own greed for it. It leads Thorin to isolate himself and his small band of companions within the thick mountain fortress. He forsakes oaths he has made to others, justifying this with the right to protect his wealth, in a way that he demands others to swear fealty to, confusing his greed for virtue. He begins to grow paranoid that men, elves and other creatures of Middle Earth may try to come claim the treasure that rightfully belongs to him, and he begins to fortify his mountain from all outsiders. Eventually his paranoia begins to turn on his own companions occupying the mountain with him. Wars that begin in our hearts eventually spread to everyone around us if we do nothing about it. War becomes an insatiable lust that chokes out all other voices of wisdom and virtue.

The story of Smaug and Thorin Oakenshield is a story of shadow-possession. They both believe themselves to be the injured party, and hence fortify the justification for war in their hearts. There is nothing quite like the intoxication of righteous indignation to draw one into war. War *is* intoxicating. This is something that most of us do not care to admit. We are ashamed of this part of ourselves and so we hide it away and pretend it doesn't exist. Still, we are fascinated by it. Like Bilbo, finding himself strangely drawn closer to the danger of the dragon in his awe of its presence, we find ourselves drawn to the theater of war as it is paraded out on the nightly news and on social media. We can't take our eyes off it. In its blindness and cruelty, war produces a zeal that overpowers all other faculties of reason, ethics, morality, virtue, compassion, or a sense of the common good. Shadow possession, just like shadow repression, always produces a crisis of the soul.

This is why war breeds more war and hate breeds more hate. Once hatred, seeded in the soul, becomes consciously or unconsciously projected into the world, it is terribly difficult to stop it from spreading, because now it has taken on a life of its own. We are no longer in control of it. The vicious cycle of violence only adds more sorrow and more pain, it does not remove it. Retributive justice may satisfy a momentary longing for revenge, but it does not bring the restorative justice that most people hope it will. Rather than laying our pain to rest, it awakens more of it because our soul knows that we have now committed the same kind of violence that we felt victimized by, even if our ego feels as though our actions were completely justified. Now, we are trapped in a cycle of pain, and the only way out is to feel it fully, make amends and let it go before it begins to erode anything left of our humanity.

Like I learned from the snake I murdered in my own dream, we must find a way to make amends for the acts of war we have already committed, both internally and externally. Making amends means that we must admit that we have caused pain, and to admit that we need to be able to confront the pain within us and hence projected outside of us. It is only in this way that we free ourselves from our pain, because when we feel it and take responsibility for it, we can turn it into compassion. Our culture today continues to teach us the opposite. Rather than being acknowledged as a virtue, experiencing pain is interpreted as a sign of weakness or pathology, and something to be avoided or fought at all costs. This fact alone shows us how sick and lonely we have become in our Western soul. We are deeply in need of the medicine that can bring the healing we long for. We are deeply in need of a peace treaty to happen within our own hearts, and in order to do this, we first need to feel our own pain; both that pain that others have caused us and the pain we have caused others. Only then is the healing of this pain possible.

We continue to deny our shadows, but our shadows have not gone away. They have not been conquered. They are bleeding out all over the place as we continue to repress them and wage war on them, and on those to whom we have projected our shadows. War, itself, is the ultimate projection of our own unresolved shadows. Our wounded pride ends up becoming nothing more than a resistance that prevents us from considering the wisdom of our own shadows and from learning how to tame the dragons that arise from them. It robs us of learning how to transform our own pain into compassion and creativity.

Eros is the love principle that must be allowed back into our hearts before they can be truly healed of war. When Eros is lost, a culture loses all of its love and its warriors and can only produce soldiers. A soldier can only follow orders, be it from a benevolent leader or a ruthless dictator. Depending on which one it is, a soldier is capable of committing either great good or great evil upon following those orders. A warrior, however, is something much more than a soldier. In many Native American traditions, a *warrior* can be understood as "fierce lover." This does not necessarily mean that the warrior is incapable of committing inhumane acts of warfare and violence, but it does suggest that a warrior is motivated by more than simple bloodlust or submission to another's desire to execute violence toward others. The warrior is motivated by this fierce love to protect others she or he loves.

One cannot become a warrior until one can show the deepest love, or Eros, for one's own people, and to do that, one must discover the deepest love for oneself first. This almost always requires some form of soul initiation involving an intense encounter with one's own shadow. One must retrieve Eros in one's own heart before it can be perceived in the hearts of others and mutually shared. Awakening to this Eros within one's own soul is part of the birthright experience. A warrior knows how to balance the tension between defending her people from genuine threats of harm and taking the time to examine her own shadows and look for resolutions to conflicts without resorting to violence, brutality or divisive rhetoric. A warrior understands the importance of compassion and the bravery necessary to practice it when the time is called for. A warrior must make the toughest decisions and be willing to feel the weight of those decisions, especially when there are no good options.

While we cannot deny the presence of war within our own hearts, we can begin listening to what our inner wars must teach us about our own unresolved conflicts, letting them guide us to what is hidden and wounded in festering parts of our own shadows. We need the creativity and active imagination of our soul's wisdom to help us navigate out of our inner wars. If we let our creativity atrophy, it tends to give way to boredom and violence. Behind the unresolved pain and discomfort that can lead to hate, which can fester into a war, may be a deep sadness or despair that has not yet found a voice we have been able to hear. It grows bitter and lonely in the dark and begins to lash out in unpredictable ways, finding places to project its wrath upon others in absence of any acknowledgment from us that it has arisen from deep within our own self-hatred.

Tolkien's terrible dragon is a symbol of all the things that surround and nurture war within our own hearts and minds when they have been left to fester in the dark for too long. The longer we sit on our own inner hatred the stronger our impulse for war becomes. Eventually that latent hatred will erupt into violence. With each act of vengeance we perpetrate upon the world, it often returns to us twice as strong. When this happens, we find ourselves in the middle of a terrible and highly destructive feedback loop. The only thing that can break that circle is our ability to connect with our own pain and allow that to be transformed into compassion. Most of us find this to be an intolerable solution, however, and so war is allowed to continue to fester and perpetuate. Ultimately, Smaug is killed while in the midst of being possessed by his unbridled rage. His inability to produce any kind of wisdom apart from his own greed and hatred becomes his undoing.

The dragons of war may be one of the most powerful and deeply unconscious dragons we can ever contend with. The irony is that we cannot find peace within our own hearts unless we acknowledge the war within them first. When we accept that we are capable of great terror, destruction, greed and violence within ourselves we can begin to bring them into the light where these parts of us have an opportunity to transform into energy for creativity and compassion rather than destruction. To reject the fiat of war within our own hearts requires a willingness to not take the paths of least resistance, of which war becomes the inevitable result. Perhaps, the reason why we find this so impossible to do has something to do with the wounds that are specific to our own Western shadow around war. Perhaps, in order to fully rid ourselves of war, we must be able to die to our own need for it first and foremost.

War may very well be irrational, but this does not mean that we must choose blindness in our apprehension of it or enact it unconsciously. Part of the purpose of this book is to teach us all how to acknowledge, accept, and embrace that which appears irrational to us with full conscious awareness and acceptance. Accepting that we have war in our hearts does not mean that we consent to wage war on ourselves or others, or that we become possessed by war. It means that we tell ourselves a difficult truth, so that we can begin the acts of inner reconciliation and transformation our soul requires of us when our own inner wars become apparent to us. We must all come to terms with the *Ares* within ourselves and know how to tame it properly before its wrath becomes all-consuming and possesses us beneath the spell of endless fear, terror and a thirst for vengeance. If we are to ever recover from our own wars, be they outer wars or wars within our own hearts, we need some healing rituals. We also need to know when to rest and take a break from engaging with our own dragons.

Part III

Inner Reconciliation and Healing

"Seeing your beauty, without extravagant self-absorption, is the first step in discovering your soul and eventually giving it the attention and care it needs."

~Thomas Moore[xxv]

Chapter 14
The Houses of Healing and the Wisdom of Sophia

Wholeness is a disorienting experience. Most of us have grown accustomed to walking through our lives in a half-way. Our first encounters with wholeness can feel strange and "unnatural." Journeys to rediscover this wholeness require some creativity and ingenuity on our part. They require us to scour the depths of the deep and the dark, exploring our own shadows. They ask us to exercise courage, wisdom and discernment in response to the dragons that appear to us. Going through the process of growing up, letting things go, making transitions, facing dragons, making room for new ways of being in the world, and waking up to the fullness of who we already are, can take its toll on us. The status quo of our own half-ness has been disrupted or perhaps been destroyed altogether. Soul work can sometimes be tough work.

Part of our soul work, we must remember, is learning how to balance the tension of opposites. Soul work does require no small amount of exertion on our part, but it also requires an ability to rest. We need a place to recover after we have gone through the juggernaut with our dragons. We must remember that, while attending to our dragons is necessary for the work of healing and wholeness, to linger in council with them for too long puts us at risk of becoming unbalanced, and we lose the tension that is important for our growth and well-being. We must give ourselves permission to take a rest from dragon work from time to time, remembering that taming dragons is only one part of soul work. Soul work also encourages us to exercise love, play and creativity, and to experience joy and gratitude. These, after all, are some of the fruits of our hard work, and if we do not allow ourselves to savor them then we are not regarding the fullness of our souls' wisdom.

For those of us who have spent much of our lives walking around in a half-way, an experience of wholeness will feel foreign and uncomfortable. This is one of the reasons why many of us reject it at first. Familiarity can often be a more powerful lure than the desire for healing and reconciliation. Our dragons play their part in pushing us forward when our soul determines that we are ready to face them. We feel inner conflict about this timing because our ego is resisting that change. As we have discovered, this is the necessary conundrum we must face in order to grow, heal, and transform. Our ability and choice to undertake this process is a part of our birthrights.

As we learn to become aware and take responsibility for our birthrights, we are better able to nourish our souls with the full healing they need, as well as tend to all our wounded parts with more tenderness and compassion. When we come to accept the inheritance of our own inner nobility, we come to understand the responsibility we have to all of the different myths we are living and the characters they produce, that reside within our psyches. Recognizing our inner nobility is how we learn to bring peace and healing to the inner kingdom.

There is a time for adventure, creativity, labor, self-improvement, and dragon-taming. These are all the elements of an active and fulfilling life. There is also a time to learn how to lay down these activities and rejuvenate our souls with peace, rest, and non-activity. Rest and recuperation are essential for our own health and well-being. To take some rest in our lives is to find a time to put down our weapons, our tools, and our ambitions, and allow ourselves to just listen to the rhythms of our body and calm our minds. Soul work requires us to learn how to pay attention to the various rhythms and seasons of life and honor them. This is not something that comes easy to modern people, who find themselves pathologically consumed with busy lives, endless deadlines, and tireless pursuits of consumption. One way or another, life forces us into moments where we must take rest, be it a dark night of the soul, or a willing and chosen respite from the many tasks and responsibilities that we have taken on in our lives.

If we have been doing some intense work with our dragons, we need to know when to withdraw and take a rest. Dragon work is not easy work, and it will take energy from us as we learn to tame and repurpose their allegiance from antagonist to ally. In some cases, the dragons we have faced are so big, exposing deep and abiding wounds, that we come away from our encounters feeling exhausted and raw. We need a place to retreat and heal before we fully incorporate the new wisdom that our dragons have brought to us back into the world.

The Houses of Healing

In *The Return of the King*, Tolkien describes a place within the great city of Gondor called the Houses of Healing. It has a very peaceful, somber, monastic feel as Tolkien describes it. It is the place in the city that the sick and wounded are sent to for care, rest, recovery and rehabilitation. It is a place where a wounded warrior can begin to reconnect with some inner peace, healing, beauty and even hope, despite having borne witness to, and suffered from, the most gruesome realities of war. It is a place for someone to put themselves back together after being broken apart. In this space, we are not looking for dragons. This is the place of rest for the soul to repair itself after it has been torn apart. Whatever dragons the future may hold for us, all belong to the future in this place. This place of healing is a place of radical awareness and surrender to the present moment, a moment meant for grace, rest and peace.

As Aragorn, Son of Arathorn, and rightful heir to the throne of Gondor, works to heal a wounded noble man of Gondor, Faramir, he makes use of a common weed not well-known for its healing powers, known as athealas. Aragorn, however, knows of its powers to heal. As a king, it is Aragorn's job to consider what others overlook in importance and value, and recognize the healing powers of that which appears unremarkable to others. This wisdom of simple things, such as the healing power of a common weed, is not lost on him. It is his birthright as a healer to hold this wisdom and knowledge. Lord Aragorn sets to his work. As he crushed the leaves their aroma was unleashed, "And straightaway a living freshness filled the room, as if the air itself awoke and tingled, sparkling with joy. And then he cast the leaves into the bowls of steaming water that were brought to him, and at once all hearts were lightened."[xxvi]

It is through a simple and overlooked element born in the common soils of the earth that Aragorn creates his healing elixir. This act is an expression of the Divine Feminine principle at work within the King. The Divine Feminine is that which heals. Aragorn has allowed himself to be in tune with his own Divine Feminine, which is what makes him prepared to accept his role as a King. He has activated his own *humus*, practicing humility in wisdom to produce healing. What a perfect metaphor to remind us of the sources of all healing, which are immanent in their nature; *grounded*; *of the earth*. Healing elixirs all have a humble origin. Deep, healing properties come from all things "earthy" or "fleshy." It reminds us that earthiness, rootedness, and groundedness, is not a source of sin or disease, but rather a source of healing and wholeness. True healing and reconciliation come from a union between the spirit and the flesh, not an imagined antagonistic divide between the two, ever at war with each other. The Divine Feminine gently urges us to re-connect with the earth once again. It woos us to become grounded, for this is where we find the roots of our healing.

A place of healing is a sacred place, and sacred places are not only confined to great cathedrals and halls of worship. Sacred places are everywhere, and most especially within our own hearts. They remain hidden to us until we are ready to acknowledge them and be fed by them. Most of us can think of at least one place or one moment in our memory where we experienced complete and utter peace, if only briefly. When we need a reference point to know what we are looking for within our own souls, we do well to remember these kinds of places in our memories. These are the places of our own houses of healing. These are our sacred places.

Symbols for healing and wholeness are archetypal. Every culture around the world has them, along with the accompanying healing rituals, and reveres them in their own way. One of the universal symbols for healing and wholeness is the circle, or a *mandala*. Mandalas are to be found in all cultures, myths and religious traditions around the world. Mandalas can symbolize that deep connectedness to the earth, the interconnectedness between all living things, the circular nature of life and death and the healing principles that are carried within that paradoxical tension between the two.

I find myself instinctually drawn to mandalas for their spiritual healing potential. Each tradition brings its own diverse elements to it, filling in the imagery of a mandala with symbols from their own traditions, ultimately meant to convey wholeness, healing, wisdom, salvation or enlightenment. In the many indigenous traditions around the world, spirit animals are symbols for healing and transformation, often displayed in mandalas or on totems meant to symbolize their wisdom and energy. Indigenous traditions are always tied deeply to the earth and have rituals that honor and worship its elements as the sources of all life.

Healing energy is archetypally expressed as a principle of the Divine Feminine. I feel it is important to again counteract the narrative regarding the feminine principle as interpreted by patriarchy; a story that regards the feminine as weak, irrational and something that must be managed or subdued in some way. Nothing could be further from the truth when apprehending the deep power of the Divine Feminine. We must be reminded often, that the energies of the feminine and the masculine belong to an archetypal realm to which all of us belong to, regardless of gender or sexual orientation. We are all called upon to recognize and actualize both feminine and masculine energies within us. The wisdom and energy of the healer is as equally as powerful and bold as the wisdom and energy of the warrior. They rely on each other's power and wisdom to function well, and we all must know how to call upon both when we need them at different moments in our lives.

The Wisdom of Sophia

Sophia, as a mythic representation of the Divine Feminine originating in the Hellenistic tradition, is a principle that is acknowledged in different ways throughout the history of Western civilization. She represents the wisdom and abundance of creation, as well as the Eros of all things created. She is the initiator of healing and reconciliation. She represents one half of the *Syzygy*, while *Logos* represents the masculine energy. Robert Powell writes, "We can conceive of Sophia and the Logos working together in the creation—Sophia as Wisdom, the plan for the shaping of creation, and the Logos as the power, the Word that informs and infuses the entire creation."[xxvii]

Sophia remains rooted in the earth in a way that the Logos, in its world of frenetic activity, does not. Logos needs to take flight to fulfill its purpose. It carries the fiery qualities of activity and the will to create and innovate. The call to creativity also requires us to listen and respond to the cooler iterations of Sophia, which reminds Logos that it is to come back to earth and reconnect with its roots after taking flight. Her creativity is of a different kind, rooted more firmly in the earth and the eco-systems of the earth that only exist and thrive together in relationship with each other. Her creativity is designed to know which elements to put together in an eco-system that help to sustain it, and which elements do not. It is her job to tend to these systems and make sure they are healthy and thriving.

Whether it is an eco-system of the earth, or the eco-system of our psyche, Sophia is responsible for healing and repairing the broken systems and relationships of that exist within them. This is the symbiotic relationship, balanced through continual paradoxical tension, that creates the wholeness that we are all seeking within ourselves, whether we are aware of that need or not. Healing and reconciliation always bring us back to the earth, keeping us grounded. When we are connected to the earth, we remember who we are. When we are connected to the ground, we find healing.

Sophia is an energy that we have not only lost in modern civilization but have been actively rejecting and persecuting for centuries. If we cannot heal that wound, we have little hope. We need only pay attention to what we are doing to our planet as we drain it of all its resources, and forever alter its climate to see just how very real this threat is. If we cannot summon the courage to bring Sophia back, then we are all in great danger of not just losing our souls, but our very lives.

Although most of us are not aware of it, whenever we are wounded enough to seek healing, consolation, reconciliation or compassion, we are moving toward Sophia. Sophia is both strong and soft. She is able to absorb all of our pain and transform it into healing, new life and purpose. Because Sophia is a principle that we have abandoned in modern, Western life, we are unaware of her presence until our own woundedness forces us to seek her out for the healing and revival we need. If we are consumed with our own half-ness, we will not recognize our need for it, and we will continue to make ourselves sick, unable to take the elixir that is right in front of us. We need a way to continually, consciously and intelligently surrender to the healing powers of Sophia beyond the mandate of our egos. Indeed, seeking her out with the same commitment we give to the Logos principle will likely save us from having to fall into moments of great woundedness and despair more often.

Sophia is a very active presence in the psyche, teaching us how to greet and tame dragons as well. Without her, we are destined to continue to slay our dragons time and time again, never having learned the important lessons of surrendering and reconciliation, which is the wisdom that Sophia provides. Sophia produces a kind of courage that is unique to her, and to which we must learn to use to face our dragons correctly. Healing requires more than just the sensation of feeling better. It requires a deeper insight into our nature that we never had before. For most of us, when tragedy hits in our lives, they can never be the same again. We might long for more innocent days when it was easier to believe in magical principles that kept us feeling safe and secure in our small worlds. When those worlds fall apart, Sophia comes to us to whisper new life and new wisdom into our spirit. We may never forget our wounds, but we need not be bound to them if we can sustain the transition into healing and receive Sophia's wisdom.

There are many gifts that we have yet to acknowledge as our birthrights as modern, Western people. These are the many gifts of the Divine Feminine presence, waiting for us to simply open our hearts and receive them. Whether we know that principle through the name of Sophia, or through other names, she is there waiting for us to accept her gifts and her wisdom. There is nothing to prove or to overcome with Her. Sophia *is* grace. Her wisdom is always there and always given freely. We need only accept it.

Sophia is the key to discovering our inner gold, the birthrights of our souls, which our dragons have been protecting for us and hiding from us until we are ready to face them and initiate the inner reconciliation process, which is a process that requires us to fall apart first, before we can be put back together.

Chapter 15
Eros and Psyche: The Art of Falling Apart

Falling apart *is* an art form, provided we can summon the courage to see it as such, and allow ourselves to surrender to it. Most of us have never been taught anything like this. In fact, most of us believe that we must do everything in our power *not* to fall apart. Falling apart may mean that I put the normal functioning of my daily life and responsibilities at risk. Falling apart may mean that I must come to terms with life as it is, rather than life as I would prefer it to be. Falling apart is certainly not comfortable and one must know how to do it with great care if one is to understand its purpose and role in helping us discover the next level of healing and wholeness that we need to keep growing and live life abundantly.

These falling-apart experiences threaten whatever ego-ideals we have originally constructed for ourselves; a "successful person," someone who "has it all together," "powerful," "healthy," "indestructible." Falling apart is dismantling our egos' presumption about our own identities, how we thought life was supposed to work, our own nature, and even faith, or belief in God. These moments can tear at the fabric of who we are, or at least how we perceive ourselves to be. There are many good reasons why we do not go looking for opportunities to fall apart and why we try to avoid the experience altogether. It hurts.

Sometimes falling apart also means that we must let go of ways of thinking or being in the world that are no longer working for us or reflective of reality. Because our tendency is to choose only one or two aspects of our psyche that we identify ourselves with, the loss of one or more as an ego-ideal can feel like a death. It is appropriate for us to grieve those losses, especially as they reveal to us deep wounds, which we had successfully been able to ignore before. The art of falling apart, however, is the doorway to new ways of thinking, being, and experiencing the world around us. It is the doorway to new life. When our paradigms and ego-ideals fail us, and most of them do eventually, we have a choice to make. Will we continue to move forward in our life, or will we stay stuck and die a slow death, the likes of which closes the door to the possibility of new life?

One might be tempted, in such a state, to avoid getting too attached to anyone or anything else in their lives. Indeed, many people do choose this in an effort to not ever have to feel too much pain, sorrow, or even anger ever again. Pain is the risk one takes when one decides to love, be it to oneself, another human being, an idea, a career, etc. Falling in love is no guarantee for avoiding the possibility of loss. It is no guarantee that we will never feel lonely again. Falling in love increases the risk. It also, however, increases our ability to learn, grow, and experience even more profound levels of joy. If we do not learn the art of falling apart, we are less likely to get back up, dust ourselves off, and summon the courage to keep living, learning, and risking love again. If we choose to stay stuck or numb to life, we risk never knowing about the gold that exists inside of us, that we must embrace if we are to accept the fullness of our lives and all the potential joy that comes with that.

Artists have experience with the art of falling apart. An artist begins with an idea that has captured her attention enough to explore it and produce something from it. The artist knows that her fidelity to her original inspiration is instrumental in setting out on a journey of discovery to produce the painting, sculpture, composition, story, etc. Along the way, the artist begins to discover different things that capture her attention, some which she did not expect. Some of these things may stay consistent with her original vision, but quite often they do not. The artist now finds herself having to abandon, perhaps, her original idea. The artist must learn to change course in order to manifest a new vision of her creation.

The artist did not make a mistake following her nose originally. She has learned to follow it, whether it stays true to the original idea, or whether it falls apart to reveal a new or different idea. This is the process of the art. The original idea was important because it brought the artist to the crossroads where the idea then had to change. The artist understands that this is how the creative process works. She would not have encountered the new idea had she not started with the original idea, even if the original idea had to be abandoned. The artist does not need to experience this process as a misstep or a failure, but rather can learn how to embrace that process as a necessary part of creativity, remaining in solidarity with the creative principle. The artist learns how to balance both the art of the will and the art of surrender in the creative process.

I believe, that the example of the artist communing with her *Muse*, and all its whims, has something important to teach all of us about how we live and experience the creativity our own lives. If we cannot surrender to greeting our own grief, sadness, and even anger around holding onto things we have carried for far too long, we will avoid the necessary falling apart that life requires of us for new growth and to live more fully into our own wholeness. The journeys of our souls are never in a straight line. There are always twists, turns, unexpected detours and the like. We may make plenty of mistakes in our lives, but when we learn how to honor those mistakes as sources of wisdom for us to continue to learn and grow, we no longer must carry around their weight in shame. Falling apart reminds us that new life is possible at any given moment, should we choose the courage to accept it.

The story of *Eros and Psyche* is a story of falling in love and falling apart. It is a myth that invites us into the archetypal journey of brokenness and restoration. As we shall see, while the story does revolve around the two characters of Eros and Psyche falling in love with each other, it has something deeper to tell us about finding our own strength and power. It teaches us that what we have most loved and adored in others, are the things we are meant most to love and cherish about ourselves. Our own inner gold. Our birthrights.

Most love stories begin with *cathexis*. Cathexis is a term used to describe an experience that is so enrapturing that one can seldom find accurate words to describe it. It is defined in the dictionary as, "The concentration of mental energy on one particular person, idea, or object (especially to an unhealthy degree)." It is a form of attachment to someone or something that produces an intense form of myopic devotion to them. In fact, the only language that ever comes close to describing the experience well is the symbolic language of myth. Falling in cathexis with someone is an act of total surrender and devotion to that one person. It is the proverbial feeling of "falling in love" that we all experience at the beginning of highly charged romantic relationships. Cathexis is an experience that also expands beyond the erotic love for another human being. It can be the expressed Eros of an idea, a philosophy, a religious or mystical experience, or some other form of epiphany that suddenly breaks into our awareness and sweeps us off our feet.

The inevitable fall from this kind of ecstasy can be quite excruciating when it happens. Our bodies are not biologically equipped to handle continuous states of such heightened ecstasy, and so this fall from it is inevitable. Many lovers do not find the love they had hoped they had with the one they are with when the excitement of cathexis wears off, and some romantic relationships end at this point. The sting of lost love is universal. One needs to look no further than the multitude of Shakespearean sonnets and modern-day pop songs about the scorn of lost love, to see just how universal and timeless this phenomenon is.

Depending on the depth of the wound of lost love, many people either consciously or unconsciously vow to never allow themselves to be open to that level of vulnerability and hurt ever again. Few of us would consciously choose the possibility of that kind of suffering. Nobody wants to be vulnerable to that kind of hurt or be made to look like a fool, and when we fall down the sometimes-steep path from ecstasy into despair, this is often exactly how it feels. The experience often changes us in ways that will leave us unable to ever feel the same way about ourselves again.

So, what are we to do when we fall apart? How are we to make sense out of such an experience? This is a critical moment in someone's life. The choice that is made can have either powerfully healing or devastating impacts on us. Some lose their lives to this kind of experience. Many others bury the hurt so far down that they become a half-person and remain that way for the rest of their lives. They have resolved to never let their true soul show again. The world went on as usual, as their world completely stood still, or crumbled altogether beneath them.

In the Greek myths and legends, the story of Eros and Psyche stands out. It is a particularly powerful myth, and one that has inspired our fascination with the concepts of passion, love, cathexis, bliss, loss, heartbreak, and brokenness to this day. "Psyche," in the Greek, means *soul*. This is important to remember as we observe different characters in the story responding to the presence of the "soul" in different ways. In the story, Psyche is the youngest and fairest of the three daughters of a king. Her beauty is so potent that it arouses the wrath of the goddess Aphrodite, who becomes jealous of Psyche's fairness. She sends her son, Eros, to pierce Psyche with one of his arrows in the hopes that she may fall helplessly in love with some vagrant or beggar, and thereby destroy any prospects for a happy marriage and a happy life.

Aphrodite does not count on her son, Eros, to fall helplessly in love with Psyche. He pierces himself with his own arrow upon the sight of Psyche and becomes a jealous lover. Psyche, hereafter, suffers from a lack of suitors to court her toward marriage, which dismays her father, because Eros is keeping them away. Consulting the gods, her father is instructed to lead her up to the top of a mountain and abandon her to her fate, which he does. In her grief, she succumbs to despair as she tries to come to terms with how alone and abandoned she feels. In the midst of her grief, the West Wind, Zephyrus, lifts her above the mountain peaks to bring her to rest in a lush, green valley below. When she awakens, she sees a palace in front of her. She spends much time exploring and roaming the palace halls but does not encounter any living creatures there.

In time, she comes to feel just as alone in the magnificent palace as she felt when first brought to the mountain. At this point, she hears a voice that whispers, "Do not be afraid, for I will not harm you. You cannot imagine how much I love you, and all I wish is for you, if you can, to love me a little in return. If you stay here in this palace as my bride, you will want for nothing—only please say you will stay!"[xxviii] The unnamed presence whispers also, a warning, "Do not ever ask me to show myself to you, for if you see me, I will have to leave you forever."

Psyche initially agrees to this arrangement, feeling quite sated by the unnamed presence which provides her with a deep love and sense of belonging that was ripped away from her when her father abandoned her on the mountain. After a while, however, she begins to miss her sisters, and makes a deal with Zephyrus to bear them to the palace to meet with her. Again, the unnamed presence issues a warning to Psyche. "Pay no attention to what your sisters tell you, for if you do, all will end between you and me."

Psyche and her sisters are relieved to see each other again. After a while, however, her sisters grow jealous of Psyche's good fortune, and begin to try to unravel the mystery behind this invisible lover. They manage to convince Psyche to go against Eros' warning to never look upon his face. Psyche is able to locate her unnamed lover in his sleep, and one night takes a lantern to his room to finally look upon his face. She is successful in her quest. When she lays her eyes on Eros, the story describes her reaction: "…the face she saw was quite the most exquisite she had ever laid eyes on, for she was looking on the face of Love itself." This is the moment with Psyche discovers that Eros is her invisible lover.

As fate would have it, a small amount of burning oil from Psyche's lamp falls on Eros' skin, which wakes him up immediately. Almost as quickly, he, the palace, and the lush green valley disappear, and once again Psyche is left alone back on top of the mountain where she had first been abandoned. Consumed by the grief of lost love, but also a new resolve and determination she had never had before, Psyche begins her quest to reclaim the love she lost. It is written, "Now began the time of her real trials, as she wandered off into the wide, wide world to seek her beloved whom she had lost through her own gullibility and foolishness."

Let us pause at this point in the story and digest what we have learned so far. The story, at the outset, seems particularly harsh on Psyche. Once again, we are challenged to move beyond the literal interpretation of the story to parse out some abstract principles that are integral to our own work toward healing and wholeness. The story of Psyche is a story which begins with the familiar comforts of innocence, which is quickly thrust into the world of awareness when her father abandons her to the wilderness. This is Psyche's first real wound and internal split. It is also her first step in her own individuation process. It is the initial loss of the childlike fantasy of the father principle, that there will always be someone there to rescue us and hold our hand when we fall and get hurt. It is a very painful realization to have and leaves us feeling lonely and abandoned. This experience, for many of us, is what instigates our first journeys out of innocence. Psyche now has the task of becoming more fully aware of herself, discovering her own giftedness and her power.

One could argue that Psyche is painfully oblivious to her own beauty at the beginning of the story, and this is true. She is completely innocent. Learning that a goddess was jealous enough of her beauty to try and curse her for it would be confusing information for her to digest. She cannot understand why her father would abandon her to the fates either, left alone, and desolate. She does not yet comprehend why she is being perceived as a threat. Left to her own devices, Psyche has no choice but to begin to open herself up to what is strong and resilient within her, but this too, requires a quest.

Remember at the beginning of the chapter when I talked about the phenomenon of falling in love? Whether it is a real relationship with another human being, an awakening to a sense of purpose and vocation in one's life, an art or skill that awakens the inner spark of genius within all of us, it grips us tightly in its passion, and we become possessed by it for a time. I described this as the process of cathexis. Not only is it a completely enrapturing and exciting experience, it is also itself a necessary part of what initiates a quest of the soul. It is what gets us out the door and into our journey, or quest. Here we have both grief and loss, comingling with passion and desire in a strange alchemical mix and paradoxical tension that must exert itself to push us out the door and onto the journey our souls have in store for us. Psyche begins to experience this in the form of her resolve to find Eros after he has disappeared.

One of the dangers of falling in love is the eventual falling apart of the façade of the perfection we feel about the person (or the idea) that we have fallen in love with. That sensation of being enraptured by the love for another, mimics in its own way, the sense of safety we originally felt from the protection of the mother and father figures in our lives when we were young. That feeling is now surrounded by a new state of bliss that we had not felt before, which makes the potential fall from this state so frightening and dangerous to so many of us. So, threatening can the prospect of losing this feeling become, that we go to great lengths to avoid its inevitability, and maintain the blissful ignorance required of us to maintain that state for as long as we can.

The problem is that eventually we lose that battle. Neither cathexis, nor blissful ignorance is a state that can be maintained, either biologically or psychologically. Eventually our curiosity will get the better of us, as it did with Psyche, and our unconscious will craft a poignant "meeting" with the fates in our lives that begin to unravel the mysteries surrounding our bliss, as Psyche's sisters do for her by instigating her curiosity. When the spell eventually breaks, we rue the disenchantment, sense of loss, and the hurt that often accompanies this experience, and find ourselves even appealing to a transcendent God or deity to remove such pain from our lives when we are suffering from it.

Grief can overwhelm us for many different reasons. When tragedy befalls our lives; when we lose someone we love, lose a job, or are estranged from family and friends whom we have loved; grief is the appropriate response. When we must grieve the loss of an ego-ideal that no longer serves our best interests, say goodbye to a way of thinking that no longer works for us, or have to move from one phase of life to the next, grieving is an appropriate response. The expression of grief, in the end, is what allows us to clear the space for something new to emerge in the soul that can eventually bring healing and joy. We do not, however, have access to this knowledge that there is a light at the end of the tunnel at the beginning, which may provide us with some hope in the midst of our grief. Psyche has had her love torn away from her, and she is in deep grief. The wound and the subsequent breaking open of the wound, however, is not the end of the story. Something new is stirring in Psyche as her resolve takes shape to leave her castle and find Eros.

As Psyche embarks on her quest, she makes her way to Aphrodite, whom she appeals to for help to aid her in her quest. Part of Psyche is still unconsciously reaching for the outer mother or father principle to aid her in her quest. She is unaware that Aphrodite is the initial source of all her troubles but is also the unwitting initiator of her soul's quest. Aphrodite sets Psyche to accomplish several impossible tasks to gain her blessing for Psyche's love affair with Eros. Again, we see the theme of impossible tasks arise in the mythological motif. Psyche, much like Vasalisa and her trial with the Baba Yaga, finds herself at the mercy of unexpected visitors that help her complete the impossible tasks, much to the chagrin of Aphrodite herself.

Psyche's final test places her on an inevitable encounter with the Underworld. Psyche cannot fully embrace her own wholeness until she encounters the things that lie in her shadows. She is on a collision course with Persephone, the Queen of the Dead. She must negotiate several barriers between herself and Persephone, all of which will kill her if she is not careful and wise. She is asked by Aphrodite to collect a part of Persephone's beauty, which she manages to accomplish with help. Persephone gives her a box that contains this prize possession. Psyche's curiosity, however, again gets the better of her, and she opens Persephone's box. "Gently, she raised the lid and peered inside. The casket appeared to be empty, but in opening it Psyche had released the potent but invisible vapors condensed within it. As they rose, she breathed them in and fell into a deep swoon, the twin of death." This is the moment where Eros re-appears and comes to the rescue to save Psyche from eternal death. No force can keep them apart now. Aphrodite's will to keep them apart is broken. She has lost. Left with no other choice, she consents to the marriage of Eros and Psyche.

It required the full death of Psyche as a helpless maiden, her original ego-ideal, left to the fates to do with as they please. It required Psyche to fall in love with her destiny, which she had to go on a quest to discover. This was journey was symbolized by both the love and heartbreak of Eros. They must return to each other with consciousness, wisdom and self-knowledge, before they can love each other appropriately and accurately. The inner marriage between the two, passionate *love* and *soul,* is symbolic of inner marriage all of us must consent to in order to accept our birthrights; learning to fall in love with who and what we really are, even in spite of all the impossible tasks that Aphrodite throws our way. We must take the journey out of innocence and into awareness, which is where we find our power. We must let our old stories, about how small and insignificant we believe we are, to die in order to claim the new stories, which are actually the original stories of our birthrights, now embraced with conscious awareness and acceptance.

The Eros within us is the part that embodies and expresses the cathexis, which is why it acts like a jealous lover. It must also be transformed into something more real and tangible if it is to continue to serve us well. Love and soul cannot really come together in a true union until after the trials of cathexis wear off, which can be a heartbreaking experience. Whether it is Eros or the Tsar-Maiden from the thrice-tenth kingdom, it is the feelings of loss, rejection, and abandonment from that which we have fallen in cathexis with that initiates our quests of the soul. It is the necessary loss to break the spell of innocence and get us moving into our own processes of individuation, designed to bring us back to our original wholeness with awareness. This is the hero's journey.

The full christening of our birthrights does not become apparent to us until we have faced the death of an incomplete and belittled version of ourselves. Again, we encounter the paradoxical theme of birth, death and rebirth. Life and death are inextricably intertwined. It is the back and forth between *Eros,* the principle of love and life, and *Thanatos,* the embodiment of death in the Greek, that we find they keys to our souls and their purpose. Rollo May writes, "The great things in civilizations come from Eros struggling against Thanatos. Thanatos without Eros would be an emptiness beyond even cruelty. But as these two great forces struggle against each other, we see the paradox of normal life."[xxix]

In the shadows, we must confront our dragons, one by one, until we are willing to take responsibility for their existence and their power, which ultimately belongs to us. In these moments, we learn to put to rest any fantasies of someone other than ourselves granting us that power. It is those parts of us that desperately need somebody else to validate our power and worth without having to take responsibility for it, that in the end, must die in order for a blessed union to take place between ourselves and our bliss, which again, is the fullness of what our souls are calling us into; the full acknowledgment of our birthrights.

All the characters in this great myth, belonging each to our own individual psyches, create the necessary conundrum, crisis, and tasks that are necessary for the soul to become more aware of itself and enter more into its own fullness. Each character in the myth can be seen as an extension of Psyche herself. Even Eros can represent the parts of Psyche that she has not yet acknowledged within herself, but is destined to fall in love with, and she cannot see Eros again until she risks the possibility of her own eternal death in the underworld.

Psyche's curiosity brought her to a dangerous place, but this ultimately was what broke the spell of the incomplete image she had carried of herself, setting her on a path to rediscover all of it. Only when she allows that old story about herself to die, is she then allowed to accept and take responsibility for her own love, passion, strength, and character now revealed to her. Only then is she able to see Eros' face for what it really is, which is the deep love she must cultivate for herself, which gives her the power to spread love in the world both wisely and passionately. There are lots of distractions and temptations on the path to inner wisdom for Psyche along the way, and they are the necessary distractions she must learn to contend with in order for her to understand the true value of her own soul.

Allowing ourselves to be broken at the right time is an essential and necessary part of recognizing the deeper purpose of our souls. The art of falling apart does not confuse moments of brokenness with a diseased or sinful nature. Brokenness is a pathway, not a destination, or an eternal state of being. Choosing to stay broken will indeed lead to all kinds of problems and ongoing neuroses that prevent us from growing up and reclaiming our original wholeness. Psyche had a decision to make when she was abandoned a second time, to either stay where she was or begin a new journey. If we get stuck along that journey of discovery, or become too enamored with one part of ourselves at the expense of all others, we inhibit the growth process toward fully discovering and surrendering to the inner genius of our soul. The soul's call on our lives keeps us moving and growing always.

Waging war on ourselves only accomplishes further fortifying the experience of division within us. We must learn the art of surrender, the art of falling apart, in order to make room to grow. In these particular moments, we will feel death. We will fall apart. When we stop fighting that inevitability and allow ourselves to surrender to the process, not only do we invite the possibility of more peace into our lives, but we begin to recognize just how strong and resilient we can be in the face of danger and uncertainty. We learn to accept death. We discover that death is simply another passageway to more abundant life.

When we are whole, then love expresses itself more fully and brilliantly from within us. We will recognize it in ourselves without needing to project it so forcefully onto others. Rather than trying to find that one person, or theory, or idea, or job or amount of money that will give us the permanent feeling of Eros, we finally learn that this Eros is foremost within ourselves and belonged to us all along. It was waiting to be discovered. Before we were conscious of Eros, it acted like a jealous lover, believing that any love we might need must obtained by theft and trickery. Eros will continue to act that way until we fully recognize and embrace it within ourselves. Eros must be transformed from the state of cathexis into real love. This disorienting journey Psyche took was preparing us for the moment when Eros was allowed to break through our unconscious defense mechanisms and bear his bright light and love for life from within our own hearts.

Chapter 16
The Alchemical Gold

The term *alchemical gold* refers to those hidden gifts or talents that lie deep within our souls but have not yet been brought into our awareness. These are our birthrights. Michael Meade writes, "Picking up a golden feather from the bird of spirit represents a breakthrough to the place where the hidden genius of a person resides and the sense of life and purpose dwell."[xxx] These are the parts of ourselves that tend to show up first through projections we place on others that we are attracted to, admire, respect or fall in love with. Because we have not yet accepted these potentialities within ourselves, we confuse them with our cathexis of others who end up carrying our gold for us.

The awareness of our own gold tends to appear in others who mirror it back to us, since most of us are unconscious about it at first. Robert Johnson writes, "If it's your gold—your soul—that is coming to consciousness, your first inkling of such a deep internal change will likely be that someone else begins to glow for you. It is your gold, but you see it in someone else; you are putting the alchemical gold on that person."[xxxi]

Johnson is describing the phenomenon of projection. We are more used to the idea of projection when it comes to recognizing the parts of ourselves that are most unpleasant to us in others, but it also works in the opposite way when we project the best parts of ourselves onto others, because do not yet see it in ourselves. Projection serves an important purpose. It provides a way for us to see ourselves, first in the image of another. Our task is to learn how to take back our own projections and incorporate them consciously into our own lives. Projection is a necessary function of human growth and understanding, without which we would not have the creation of the great myths, themselves projections, that mirror back to us the deepest truths of our human nature and experience.

Projection is something that we all do, and if we can learn to become aware of it when we are doing it, then projections serve us as a great source of wisdom and insight. Projections only cause us trouble when we choose to remain unconscious about them and fail to take personal responsibility for them. The projection of our unrecognized gold offers us an opportunity to come to terms with something beautiful within ourselves that we have not yet been made aware of. It mirrors back the potential that resides within us that perhaps we never thought possible, nor ever even considered before.

There is a reason why our gold is not immediately apparent to us. Without a journey of discovery, out of innocence and into consciousness to recapture it, we would never understand its true power and purpose, and we may be more likely to take its value for granted. Even though our gold has always been there from the beginning, the paradox of the journey to rediscover it is the necessary tension that fuels our growing awareness that there is something important for us to retrieve. Discovering this inner gold is also an important part of the healing process when we have been wounded.

When we allow our own life to speak from within us, we are connected to our own gold. We are often not aware of our own gold until we recognize it first, in the face of someone who is carrying it for us. This is the projection. What we are truly admiring or falling in love with is the reunion with our own gold, even if we are not aware that this is what is happening. Love and the sharing of love does serve the purposes of companionship and connection with others, but it also serves the purpose of opening us up to see what is truly valuable about ourselves and learn to embrace those parts of us without reservation.

We never stop having opportunities to work with our own projections. One should not have the goal of ridding oneself of all projections, but rather be an active and willing participant with them, recognizing their usefulness as tools by which we learn and understand and value ourselves more fully. So long as we are willing to recognize our projections for what they are and are ready and willing to take responsibility for them, we can freely participate in our own soul's wisdom and abundance, and relish in its creativity.

In this sense, we allow the phenomenon of projection to be an important part of what makes life sweet and interesting for us, rather than a confounding and lamentable human foible to overcome. Rather than frustrating our efforts to realize our own deep inner wholeness, projections play an important role in helping us continually awaken to our inner wholeness. Projections can help us initiate the necessary journeys with the necessary conundrums we must face at just the right times. When we are not busy fighting or ignoring our projections, they become useful guides and companions. They tell us more about ourselves than whatever self-imposed identity our egos are protecting for us.

Imago (Soul Images)

Imago is the Latin word for "image." In traditional psychoanalysis, the term imago is used to describe the original mother and father image imprinted upon us from birth. The term *Imago Dei* comes from the Christian tradition, a term that simply means "image of God," referring to the divine imprint of God within the soul of every person. Hindus use the term *Namaste* when greeting others, a term that signifies the recognition of the divine in me bowing to the divine in you. Other forms of mysticism celebrate the idea that, deep within, we can acknowledge and honor the image of the divine within us. Different traditions have come up with some very creative ways of recognizing and revering the many images of the soul, or imagoes.

The term *imago*, I believe, can also be used synonymously with the word *soul*. An *imago* is a projection that acts like a mirror, feeding back to us the deepest truths of who we really are. Imagoes are myths in action. The Soul, the Psyche, or the Self are all representations of the totality of an individual, and all of the parts that contribute to the whole desire to make themselves known to us through soul images. The soul, far more expansive and vaster than our waking consciousness, tends to communicate with us most powerfully in images and symbols that draw us in for reasons that may not be immediately obvious to us. These images are appealing to the immediate experience of our intuition before our rational mind has a chance to parse out their meaning. Learning how to live with soul images means learning how to sit with them for longer periods of time, before we attempt to discern them.

Our souls are much wiser and older than we are. Our souls remember important information that our egos quickly forget. Maya Angelou once stated that we are far more likely to remember how someone made us feel, than what they may have said to us. This is evidence of what I like to call *soul-memory*. Part of what happens when we begin to regard consciously the images from our unconscious soul is that we remember things we had long since forgotten, almost like an old, familiar fragrance that immediately takes us back to a place and time where we felt peace, rest and even a sense of childlike wonder. Our soul remembers these important events, images and details and shares them with us at the appropriate moment, giving us exactly what we need, exactly when we need it. Our souls are teaching us that they are abundant and trustworthy. If we learn to listen and let them guide us, and if we have learned how to do our shadow work, we discover that we are safe and trust-worthy as well.

Soul images sometimes speak a language of their own and must often be experienced before they can be understood, if they can be fully understood at all. As a matter of fact, our attempt to grasp them cognitively too soon may send these parts of our soul back into hiding. This is not to say that our intellectual capacities are bad or wrong. It simply means that they have their proper use and limits, just as the deeper feeling functions do. Again, if we embrace that we live in a world of paradoxical tensions, we can easily recognize how both faculties of reason and intuition are important, and how both bring mutual benefit to each other.

Our job is not finished once we learn to accept and embrace our own gold. The next task is to manifest that in the world. Here is where we will learn how to better balance the paradoxical tension between the desire of our souls and the ego-ideals we carry. This is what it really means to be authentic. We accept ourselves as we are when we make the decision to act in this life authentically and with purpose. We learn, once again, how to listen, trust, and respond to the deep rhythms of our lives, and honor them instead of fighting or ignoring them. How we choose to listen is very important. Sometimes, we need to negotiate the needs of our souls, which tend to be more patient than the needs of our egos. The ego is always concerned about having enough. It tends to act out of its own fears of scarcity, while the greater soul is rooted in a spirit of abundance, grace, and deeper wisdom. As such, it is not prone to accommodate whatever demands the ego may want to impose upon it. When we seek the wisdom of our own souls, we must seek it in a spirit of humility and often, patience.

When Joseph Campbell talks about following your bliss, he is not talking about chasing trivial pursuits of wealth, happiness or momentary comfort. By bliss, he is referring to the deepest desires and purposes of one's soul. He writes, "The whole idea is that you've got to bring out again that which you went to recover, the unrealized, unutilized potential in yourself... You are to bring this treasure of understanding back and integrate it in a rational life."[xxxii] A vocational life, as opposed to a career or a profession, is centered in the place where our bliss meets with our work in the world, and informs our work in the world. All of us have several vocational callings that we discover over the course of a lifetime, and the way we begin to recognize these vocational callings is through our own soul work.

While I believe the concept of the soul to be archetypal in nature, the idea of it can sometimes become a barrier for some. In an increasingly secularized Western world, the word *soul* often carries too many religious implications with it to be taken seriously and regarded wisely by those who claim no religious or spiritual connections. Another dilemma, as Thomas Moore recognizes, is that the word soul can mean so many different things to different people. In this text, I adopt Moore's understanding of the soul when he writes,

"Soul is not a thing, but a quality or a dimension of experiencing life and ourselves. It has to do with depth, value, relatedness, heart, and personal substance."[xxxiii]

Soul, then, is the expression of an experienced wisdom and is expressed most potently in the language of myth and symbol, which is more than a significant enough barrier for modern people to be able to consider. After all, we cannot scientifically measure soul any more than we can scientifically measure imagination, yet we all know what an imagination is and how it is used. We can measure brain activity from people who are participating in what many consider to be mystical experiences, prayer or spiritual ecstasy, but that gets us no closer to understanding or quantifying the actual experience itself.

And yet, in spite of all this, the idea of the soul still captures our imaginations and proves to be very powerful. It is the source of our deepest values. It informs how we behave, how we experience ourselves, and how we come to terms with our own sense of purpose in the world. Whether there is such a thing as a soul, I believe it will continue to elude our full understanding and grasp of it. Perhaps that is where its power lies. It is one of those things that exerts a lot of power over us but disappears the second we try to define or quantify it in some way. The soul refuses to be pinned down, as it were. The best any of us can do, I believe, is to describe its impact on us, in much the same way one attempts to describe the impact of a great work of art. We must allow ourselves to explore the ancient idea of the soul, and all the ways that we can begin to listen to its wisdom in our daily lives.

Learning to listen to these deep soul voices that come from within us is a part of what it means to touch the alchemical gold. One of the dangers in reacting to our own gold in someone else is that we may take the projection literally, and believe that what our deepest soul wants is to *be* the person who is carrying our own gold around for us. While that person may exhibit many of the personal qualities we admire, and even wish to emulate, it would be very foolish to believe that we are inevitably meant to be doing the same exact things in life as the person who has been carrying our gold around for us. To fall into that trap might be a costly misinterpretation of how we learn to recapture projections that we have put onto other people. Even though someone may be carrying our gold for us, it is important to remember that they are still an individual person with their own path to take, and their own soul calling. They have likely also projected their own gold onto someone. Our task is not to mimic the person carrying our gold for us but discover what our gold has in mind for us to do as our own person with our own path to follow.

To stay enraptured by our gold in the face of someone else, without learning to take it back, is to repeat the doom of *Echo* and *Narcissus*, each cursed in some way to love that which is unobtainable to them. Echo can only mimic the words of others, and so cannot summon any words of her own. Narcissus cannot love any other but that of his own projection, which he discovers in the reflection of a pool. Every time he tries to touch his own reflection, it disappears. Neither of them is capable of loving themselves as they are, but only the projections they have cast of themselves, which they prove unable to take back and discover it within themselves. The tale of Echo and Narcissus is a cautionary one. It reminds us just how important soul work is, and specifically the work of recognizing our own gold in the faces of others and learning how to take it back. When we fail to do this, as both Echo and Narcissus did, we can easily fall into despair. We are trying to live someone else's life rather than our own, and predictably, we will continually feel as though we can never measure up to that person.

Despair, in some ways, may be the opposite of being fully awake and conscious. Despair is what sets in when we cannot take our own gold back and are not even aware that we are supposed to. We are forever comparing ourselves unfavorably to other people who appear to have everything that we wish to possess but believe ourselves to be incapable of having. When we begin, however, to recognize our own soul and the gold it wishes to produce, *within us*, there we arrive at a moment of wholeness that we had never known before. We find ourselves a little sturdier and a little less wary of things. We find ourselves able to savor the moments of our lives more fully. Yes, we had to pass through a dark night of the soul, face some very fierce dragons, and reclaim for ourselves our potential and our abilities that we had unconsciously asked others to carry for us; but eventually we come to terms with the existence and importance of our own gold, just as we have with our own shadows. We no longer need to fight and repress either of them. Rather we know how to welcome them as vital parts of our own psyches.

When we can accept all the parts of ourselves, made of both light and shadow, then we are able to enact the birthrights that have belonged to us from the very beginning. We become less concerned with what other people have done and what they are doing, and we become more present to ourselves and our own work. We begin doing things we've never done before. This is when we begin to embody and enact the deep vocations that our souls have in store for us. This wisdom may feel new to us, but it is not new to our souls. We were drawn to it, because somewhere unconsciously, we already recognized it. These are the gifts that the soul has been waiting to reveal to us since the beginning.

When we have successfully met ourselves at the crossroads between light and dark, masculine and feminine, weak and strong, and other paradoxical tensions, we must learn to balance, we have arrived at those meaningful moments when we finally recognize and embrace the gifts of our own souls. These crossroads are the places where we learn the paradoxical tensions, we must balance to stay alive, awake, and keep life savory! These are also the gifts that we learn to give to the world around us. They are the truest gifts, because they have arrived into the world from within ourselves, as we truly are.

Chapter 17
Reconnecting to Our Inner Wilderness

A significant element of our experience of inner fragmentation and isolation comes from a disconnection with the wilderness, both within us and outside of us. We have forgotten that our very own DNA is tied to lands of our ancestors. As we continue to work hard to "conquer" the natural world, we continue to work toward further inner fragmentation within ourselves and further outer fragmentation with each other. The earth and its wilderness are what tie us together, for we all belong to the land. If we were to recognize and accept this truth, we would treat each other very differently, and our decisions to engage in technological progress would be informed by very different values.

As noted at the beginning of the book, our dragons are creatures of the wild, and one of the reasons we are so threatened by them is because they remind us that we too belong to the wild, the land, and to each other. As we continue to neglect, destroy, and pillage our natural resources, so we do to ourselves, and the harder we ignore or fight this truth, the bigger and scarier our dragons become to wake us up and grab our attention. The more investment we have in a divide and conquer approach to nature (including our own human nature), the more we choose to fight or ignore these dragons. Our world is enough, and we are enough, but we choose to fight this truth, fight each other, and fight with ourselves as a result.

The politics of division and scarcity are the politics of the Half-Man and his world. His is a world that is reaching, perhaps, the apex of its power and its resources to sustain that power. There is a great, unconscious fear of the loss of that power that those who hold it cannot recognize, because to do so would be too great of a cost for them to consider. For those of us who are paying attention, the world is currently writhing in chaos and fear as some of its long-dormant, collective dragons are finally beginning to break through the surface and façade of omnipotent human power and control over nature. As the fear edges closer to the surface, the more brutally and aggressively those in power fight back, unable as they are, to recognize and contend with their own dragons.

While these power dynamics have existed since the dawn of our species, and hence are nothing new, what *is* new are the technological capabilities we have attained as a species, providing new ways for us to engage in destructive forms of conflict, including the weaponization of media and social media. We have more power than we have ever had before to wipe ourselves out as a species with remarkable speed, efficiency and brutality.

This is a dangerous time in the history of our species. If we cannot learn how to tame and befriend our own inner dragons, we cannot tame our collective dragons, and if we cannot come to terms with our collective dragons, then many more people are likely to get hurt or killed as a result. For just as we have learned to attack ourselves when we see parts of us we do not like, we have learned to attack each other too. It is our own, rejected projections that we attack, and our projections take the form of dragons which we believe must be slain because they threaten our willingness to collude with the resignation of our own "half-ness."

The wilderness reminds us that we are not in charge, and when we are not in charge, this allows us to belong to something. The very first place we need to learn to belong again is the wild. It is the wilderness that teaches us the principle of belonging, first within ourselves and secondly with each other. Without one we cannot do the other, and the wilderness embodies this principle, reminding us that everything in nature is dependent on everything else around it to exist.

When we belong, we begin to pay attention to what and who we belong to, and when we pay attention, we learn to notice things that we have not noticed before. On a recent trip to Scotland, I couldn't help but notice just how green everything was there, but to simply describe Scotland as "green" is to do it a grave injustice. What I began to notice when I allowed myself to take the time and feel like a part of the landscape there, was just how *many* shades of green there were, which would be more than I could count. In that moment, I experienced both awe and gratitude, which only occurred when I allowed myself to be connected to the vibrant variations of green that permeated that land.

This is another thing the wilderness teaches us. We can experience neither awe nor gratitude without the experience of belonging, and in order to belong, we must first recognize not only the value of our own existence but also the value of others. To attempt to disregard the value of one in exchange for the other is how both are eventually destroyed. If we cannot value ourselves, we will be unable to value others and vice versa. For, once we choose not to belong to something, we choose not to see it; and once we choose not to see it, we no longer feel beholden to it.

This is how racism, classicism, fundamentalism, xenophobia, homophobia, and many other forms of division and illusions of supremacy are created and nurtured, and the greater the threat becomes to our illusions of power, control and autonomy, the greater the violence inflicted on any group with which we have grown accustomed to calling the "other." In creating the "other," we strip those to whom we have commissioned this title of their humanity. This, ultimately, is what allows us to commit acts of inhumanity upon others without any awareness of how we are committing violence toward ourselves as we inflict it upon others.

Our dragons, being themselves creatures of the wild, are designed to foil and disrupt our illusions and delusions of power and control, based on the ego-ideal of a rugged, individualistic autonomy. This value is a monument to our "half-ness." Reconnecting ourselves to the wild is how we begin to recapture our wholeness once again. Our dragons bring the wild to us when we roundly reject all opportunities to reconnect with the wilderness within ourselves. A reconnection to the wild teaches us that what needs to be given up is not that which makes us who we are, but rather that which continues to *separate* us from who we are. Who we are—that which makes us human—is a sense of belonging, and that sense of belonging extends between us and our inner world and those to whom we belong in the outer world, which includes our home, this planet Earth. Our very human nature *is* relationship.

In living out our illusions and delusions of autonomous power over others, we have lost the ability of discernment between that which is truly sacred and truly profane. That we have created false idols and false stories of ourselves and regarded them as sacred is of no consequence to the dragons of the wilderness, intent to trample our false idols as impediments toward recapturing our original wholeness. They exist to destroy that which we have bestowed the title "sacred," unjustly, disingenuously and often inhumanely.

To re-engage with the wilderness is to reprogram ourselves, so to speak. It serves to undo whatever we have learned to exalt as sacred from the world of the Half-Man and reconnect us to our own inherent wholeness. It is in the wilderness that the rejected and outcast spirit of the Divine Feminine awaits our reunion with Her once again, and She appears to wait with an endless, divine patience. It is in the wilderness that we teach ourselves how to belong again. It is in the wilderness that we learn to regard that which is not in our control—that which is untamed—as sacred once again.

Dragon work is one way that we connect with that which is wild and untamed within us. When we allow ourselves to reconnect with our own wild, we discover the beauty and depth of our true nature as creatures of inherent wholeness and belonging. The wilderness transforms us not into something other than who we are, but reawakens us to what is, and has been, the essential truths of our human nature from the very beginning. Once again, it appears that this sacred process of forgetting and remembering, death and re-birth, is the fire with which we continue to grow and deepen; *The Fire That Never Dies.*

When we confront, take council with, and repurpose our relationship with our own dragons, we give ourselves an opportunity to roam the wild, internal landscapes of our souls; places that we had never dared brave before. When our dragons no longer need to be our enemies, they become our wise companions, providing us with the energy, courage, vitality, and curiosity to explore everything that the wilderness of our own souls holds for us.

As with all adventures we must expect, and be prepared for tough moments, unexpected detours and sometimes ferocious odds. Again, we are reminded in each of these moments that we are not in control. Befriending our dragons teaches us how to stop fearing our own fear, which allows us to confront those fears, take council with them, learn about those parts of ourselves that desperately need healing (perhaps that we were not even aware of), and bring inner reconciliation to places we had long since abandoned, but have not abandoned us. This is the language of the wilderness. It does not abide by our expectations and ego-ideals. It is not corralled into safe categories that we can manipulate, nor is it concerned about our own ideas of readiness or timing.

When I was standing in, and amongst, the countless shades of green in the Scottish wilderness, I knew that I was deeply connected to something much larger than myself. Discovering my apparent smallness in this wilderness and the vast universe in which it resides was not an invitation for me to question my inherent value or significance. Nor did it leave me feeling lonely and isolated. Rather, it was an invitation for me to learn how to love and honor myself accurately, which is to recognize my own sense of worth and belonging. The wilderness teaches us this humility. Remember that to be "humble" means to regard oneself accurately; to tell the truth about oneself. Our smallness in the universe does not determine our value or significance. To suggest this is to collude with the ethics of the Half-Man's desire for power and control, which can only measure the value and worth of something in proportion to its size and power.

The healing power of the wilderness is its ability to recalibrate our souls, so we reawaken to our own inherent value and worth as creatures of belonging. It is to the wild places of the earth that we belong, and so it is to each other, and ourselves, that we belong. Our dragons are a part of that wilderness as well, reminding us of the inherent wilderness of our own souls. We must learn to take council with them with wisdom and humility, as we must also learn to appropriately take council with all the many parts of ourselves that make us human and reflect the nature of our belonging within our individual souls, and with each other.

Part IV

Taming Our Dragons:
The Praxis

"Challenge is a dragon with a gift in its mouth. Tame the dragon and the gift is yours."

~Noela Evans[xxxiv]

Chapter 18
The Healing Art of Curiosity

Curiosity is the attitude and the stance which we must learn to take when we approach our dragons. They are protecting an inner treasure that is meant to serve, edify, heal and bring us back to our own wholeness. Contrary to the many dragons in our Western myths, that hoard treasure out of greed or malice, the dragons of our inner psyches are meant to serve a very different function. They are the supreme protectors of our inner treasure and will not allow us access to that treasure if we approach them with our own greed and malice.

So, what is this treasure that our dragons are protecting for us? The treasure is the most vulnerable parts of who we are that we have rejected and abandoned. Our deepest and most basic desires, needs, fears, hopes, and dreams are the treasure that our dragons are protecting, and not for themselves, but for us when we are finally ready to acknowledge, accept and take responsibility for them.

Developing curiosity about ourselves and practicing that curiosity is a very different task from self-improvement or social ladder-climbing. While both of those may be necessary for us to learn in a world that demands those skills of us, they each begin with the premise that "I am not enough." They operate under the assumption that there are parts of ourselves that are undesirable or a liability to us in some way. The harder we work to hide, bury or rid ourselves of these more vulnerable parts of ourselves, the more we feed our own shame, which tries to protect the feelings of worthlessness or fear we develop about these wounded places.

As mentioned previously in the book, curiosity is the antidote to pervasive shame and fear, which likes to hide and protect us from our own vulnerability. Curiosity points us in the opposite direction and poses a very different kind of task for us. Cultivating our ability to become more curious about ourselves invites us into a different *experience* of ourselves, and it is in this experiential place that we find the "cures" that we have been looking for. Curiosity invites us to get out of our own heads, with all its schematics, procedures, distractions, and strategic defense mechanisms, and simply enter the sanctum of our own souls.

There is where we will find our treasures, guarded by the dragons that have been tasked to protect them for us, until we are ready to accept them with grace and gratitude. We need simply greet them with curiosity (as opposed to shame, suspicion or hostility) to gain their trust. Only then will they allow us to see the treasure that has been lying in wait for us. Only then can our dragons trust us to value that treasure and use it for what it was meant for rather than attempt to possess, control, or destroy it. It is in these moments that we must learn to check our egos at the door and practice the courage to be vulnerable to ourselves.

Our dragons honor and revere courage, because they know that vulnerability is a prerequisite for its purpose and practice. If we are not vulnerable or afraid, we have no need for courage. Courage presupposes a certain kind of humility on our part in order to practice it accurately. Courage also presupposes the recognition of value and worth. We would not need to utilize courage to retrieve something that has no value for us.

We need not spend hours or days dreaming up strategic ways of confronting our dragons. This impulse betrays an attitude of fear and even aggression towards our dragons. We cannot fool them with this, because they can smell it, and will greet our fear and hostility in like fashion. Remember that if we treat our dragons as an enemy to be slain or conquered, we can expect them to behave as an enemy. If, rather, we can learn to approach our dragons with courage, humility and curiosity, then we can also expect them to respond in kind. The only thing we are required to do is to humble ourselves, approach our dragons with curiosity (and in good faith), and simply ask them to reveal what we need from them.

Not all of the wounds we carry within us are problems to be solved. Many of them are treasures to be revealed and cherished. Most of the time the reason we experience these vulnerable parts of ourselves as wounds is because they have been mistreated, often first by other people early on in our lives, and then eventually by us as we have learned to hide them from the threat of harm from others. We learn to "protect" ourselves by punishing and burying these wounded places deep down inside of us.

It is no wonder then, that practicing the art of curiosity requires so much courage. We must learn to become revealed to ourselves and cherish who we are, rather than lament over what we are not, and continue whatever crusades we have begun to rid ourselves of these troublesome parts through aggression or abandonment. In this way, we can recognize clearly that our dragons are a gift to us, for they prevent us from successfully accomplishing the goal of destroying or abandoning ourselves completely. They teach us that the only way we can find healing and wholeness is through a profound acceptance of the totality of who we are. Self-knowledge is not an act of conquest. It is rather an act of surrender to what is true about us.

Getting curious about ourselves requires some kind of regular practice on our parts. It is not enough to simply entertain this idea in our heads. We must find ways to enact this curiosity in our daily lives, learning to be more fully embodied in all of their moments. Practices of mindful meditation, where we learn to observe all of the different thoughts and feelings we have with less judgment and less attachment, can also serve to help us learn how to get curious about them and form different relationships with them along the way.

Acts of creativity often serve as very powerful vessels for our curiosity, as we learn ways to express different parts of ourselves through art, music, storytelling, dance and many other mediums of expression. Engaging in these acts of creativity serves the same impulse within us that drove us to write the ancient stories and myths that we stay connected to even today. These acts of creativity soften the barriers we put between ourselves and our more vulnerable and wounded places, giving them a voice and teaching us something important about ourselves by doing so.

Writing is an act of creativity as well, if we choose to regard it as such. Writing things down is also a physical act. It requires the cooperation of our bodies to execute, and the more we can get our bodies involved in the process of curiosity and creativity, the more effective our efforts to engage with these vulnerable parts of ourselves will be. A journaling process allows us to take things out of our head and put them on paper. It becomes a little easier for us to see them concretely and interact with them. This further allows us to learn how to develop better relationships with these vulnerable and wounded parts of ourselves as well, as we learn to shift from abandonment or attack, to courage and compassion as way to approach and enter into a dialogue with them.

Practicing the art of curiosity is a way for us to experience and express joy and gratitude. Curiosity teaches us how to celebrate our lives and the gifts we all have within us that are simply looking for an opportunity to express themselves in the world. When we allow them to speak and even guide our lives, we become capable of experiencing joy and greeting the world anew.

Our Western heritage has provided us with many doctrines about how our human nature is inherently corrupt, flawed and even evil, teaching us that we must all become "better" than what we are. All of these doctrines teach us to look outside of ourselves for the keys to our salvation. The art of curiosity points us in the opposite direction—to have the courage to come back to ourselves and explore what is already there—to discover the healing, the medicine and even the salvation we have been looking for. Our task in life is not to figure out how to become less human, but how to become more human, and becoming more human sometimes involves taking the hero's journey away from our home (ourselves), where we left our innocence behind, only to return back home with knowledge and awareness. Often, we must take such a journey to be able to recognize the value or even the existence of what we already have and already know.

Practicing the art of curiosity is an expression of the journey of the soul. Our soul longs to travel and learn, not because it lacks what it needs, but because it finds joy and value in discovering new things and trying new things. It likes movement and requires an ability to challenge our impulses to stay put or hold onto something for too long. It wants to grow by its very nature, which means it requires our ability to stretch beyond our comfort zones and what has grown familiar to us. One of the gifts we receive by making peace with our dragons is that we create space within ourselves to explore and learn from a place of joy rather than a place of urgent anxiety that we are "missing" something important that we need but do not yet have.

It is important to remember that our souls have access to all that is hidden and underground within us, and all that is hidden and underground in what Carl Jung would call the "collective unconscious." By virtue of this, our souls are older and wiser than we are. Our souls know what we need long before our ego consciousness becomes aware of it. When we approach ourselves with curiosity and compassion, we enter into the realm of the soul, and we learn to trust it a little more each time we choose to listen to what it has to say.

Our souls carry the images and imprints of all of the dragons, allies, strange creatures, characters, and anomalies that get projected into our myths and stories. Whatever images hold power for us are the images that we are meant to see and learn how to listen to. These images will be different for every single person, because we are all unique in many ways. Our souls teach us to trust our own wisdom, even as we are learning to rely on the wisdom and feedback of others. Occasionally, these will be at odds with each other, which is why we must continue to learn the practice of courage over and over again. In the end, only we can decide for ourselves the paths we must follow, even if those paths may lead us away from the good advice and good intentions of others.

We must remember that practicing the art of curiosity also brings us the potential for immeasurable joy and celebration of life. Yes, it often requires a courageous compassion on our part to unlearn all of the barriers we have put between ourselves and the vulnerable parts of ourselves, but the treasure we receive from having done this work is why we choose to pursue it. Our own gold is meant for us to humbly acknowledge, receive and take responsibility for. When we are finally able to accept our own gold, we begin to feel at home within ourselves. Suddenly, we may begin to recognize that many of the things we considered "problems" that needed to be solved are no longer problems.

For most of us, we need to create the time and the opportunities to heal our relationships with these wounded and vulnerable parts of ourselves, which means that we have to learn more about the dragons that are protecting them and what they need us to know. The dragon can be thought of as more of the outward manifestation of the wound itself, and in that sense, they are one in the same. As we learn to dialogue with our dragons, they change over time because we are beginning to create a safe space within ourselves to allow the wounded parts within us to finally grow up and begin learning more about this world that we inhabit. As these parts of ourselves heal, discover purpose, and grow more confident, the dragons that protect them can utilize their energies in other ways beyond simply protecting our wounded and vulnerable parts.

Taking the time to better understand not only the nature of our dragons, but the nature of the relationship they have with us and with the other parts of ourselves requires some curiosity and some action on our part. In the next chapter, I will explore a journaling process which can help us learn how to do this. The journaling process teaches us the difference between all of the different parts of ourselves and the stories that these parts may be carrying about us, and what our task is when we confront our dragons and the stories they are telling.

Chapter 19
Taming Dragons: The Inner Work

The dragons we face throughout our lives can often feel punishing and exhausting. The longer we ignore them the more intense these feelings become. If there were no "pearl of great price," as it were, for our efforts in the end, not many of us would find it worth our time to engage them. In fact, many modern people have decided that this is the case, abandoning hope that there is a pearl of great price to be found.

We certainly have not been provided with a modern language or many modern rituals to teach us to explore the depths of our souls and discover what resides there. Most of our modern religious, political, and economic institutions are still too invested in the total conquest or suppression of the Shadow to be of good support to us when it comes to dragon-taming, and so, we are forced to look within our own hearts and souls and trust that they know what they are doing. Learning the language of our shadows and that of our dragons is an important first step.

Naming a dragon means first, to accept that it exists, and second, to accept that it has something of value to teach us, help us reconcile, and ultimately to cherish. Once we have invited the dragon into our inner sanctum, however, our task is not over. It has just begun. It is only as we learn to take council with our dragons repeatedly and over time that we earn their loyalty and willingness to lend us their gifts to use in life-giving ways. Trust must be built, and trust requires an active and ongoing relationship. It will take time for us to adjust to allowing our dragons to be fully accepted as a part of our inner council as well. We will have days where we have more tolerance for their presence and other days when we will have less. We will have moments when we choose to treat our dragons as enemies again. Hopefully, if we have been building a good working relationship with them over time, they will remind us (not always gently) that we were the ones that initially invited them to come in and share their wisdom with us, and that we must take the steps to rebuild trust whenever it has been broken.

The wisdom and vitality that we receive from our dragons, and the ongoing partnership between them and the other parts of our psyche, is "the pearl of great price." It is the experience of wholeness with awareness, of reconciliation with purpose and a flourishing access to our own creativity as we learn to heal our inner woundedness and retrieve more of our own inner gold. The pearl of great price is the recognition and acceptance of our birthrights. No one can ever take that away from us. Even if we do not always live up to our own inner royalty, we now find ourselves on the other side of innocence once we claim those birthrights. We cannot deny their existence or put the proverbial genie back in the bottle.

To tame a dragon is to take responsibility for its power, its nature, and its gifts to us. It requires an ability to practice the tensions of the paradox as we learn to hear from all of the different parts of ourselves. This does not guarantee us a life without trouble, a life of uninterrupted peace or even a life free of frustration and pain. It does mean, however, that we acquire a valuable ally with the power of the dragon at our side when we need its strengths and gifts. The gift of the dragon, as with all of the different parts of the psyche, is the gift of the yearning of the soul being made manifest to us. It brings forth the necessity of our purpose, mission and vocation. It is the voice of emancipation from old or false stories about ourselves that no longer serve any life-giving purpose. It brings the wisdom necessary for us to surrender to the ongoing work of uncovering unknown layers of ourselves for the duration of our entire lives. Dragon work is soul work.

Our Stories

All of the different parts of our psyches carry with them stories about ourselves that we have collected over time. It is vitally important that one learn to make a distinction between a part of one's own psyche and whatever story that part has been carrying. Confusing the two makes it very difficult to do the work of inner reconciliation, as we attempt to rid ourselves of a part of ourselves, rather than harmful story about us that this part has been carrying for us. Once we understand that we have rejected a part of ourselves because it is carrying a harmful story that we have unconsciously accepted as true about us, we can learn how to eventually repair that broken relationship while teaching these parts of ourselves to let go of the harmful stories we have made them carry for so long.

A good example of how this works is to take a look at the motif of an abandoned child, which is a part of the psyche that most (if not all) of us carry in one way or another. Perhaps that child felt abandoned because when we were children ourselves, we fell victim to neglect, abuse, bullying, or more common forms of dehumanizing behaviors and accusations from others that tried to tell us that we have little to no worth. We may learn, in these moments, that the needs and desires we had for love and acceptance when we were young have become a threat to our getting love and acceptance later on, and that it is better not to show them. Hence, we too, learn how to abandon and neglect our own frightened children within us. Our instinct, when and if we allow ourselves to feel the woundedness of this part of us later on in life, is to want to continue to abandon and neglect these parts of ourselves. Our task, rather, is to learn how to listen, love, encourage, and protect these wounded and frightened parts of ourselves. It is only when these parts of us learn that our desire to show them love and compassion is real that they learn to trust us once again, and it is only then that we can convince these parts of ourselves to let go of the stories they have long been carrying that we are of no inherent worth or value.

What we learn in this process is that it is false or inhumane stories about ourselves that we have been carrying that we are meant to let go, not the wounded part of our psyches that have been carrying it. *The Fire That Never Dies* does not burn us away, but rather these old stories of ourselves that have outlasted their usefulness or purpose, and no longer serve the best interest of our own growth and healing.

Not all stories that we have been carrying about ourselves are harmful or untrue. Some stories may in fact, be very useful, but only for a period of time, in which it becomes important for us to let them go to create room for new stories that are better suited to wherever we happen to find ourselves in life at the moment. It is important also to recognize that we remain unaware of other stories about us that are potentially very life-giving, but we have not allowed yet into our own awareness, for various reasons. Because our ego has chosen one predominant story about us that we have accepted and chosen to live out, it serves to reason that most of the other stories we carry remain unknown to us. Our dragons appear to show us either unresolved or purposefully suppressed stories we have chosen to reject. Because of this, our tendency is to want to "kill the messenger," so to speak, rather than recognize a distinction between the story and the one who bears it. The stories we carry within us have a more transitory nature to them than the different parts of our own psyches.

As already noted, some of these stories we discover about ourselves are very life-giving, and we benefit greatly from. It is important that we support and uphold them in our lives for as long as they are serving us well. Some of our stories are incomplete and require us to finish writing them. Some stories are suffering from wounds that need some healing and reconciliation before they can be fully actualized within us. Then there are the stories that we carry around within us that need to die. Either they have outlived their usefulness, or they are actively harmful to us in some way, preventing us from recapturing the fullness of our own inner gold and our own wholeness. These are the stories that our dragons are most likely to bring to our attention when we find ourselves unwilling or unable to let go of them ourselves.

To tame a dragon is to repurpose its antagonistic energy into a life-giving resource within us that we learn to honor and rely on. We need its energy to discover, repurpose or put to death the different stories we have been telling about ourselves. This is part of how we turn our dragons into allies and rely on them to help temper other aspects of our souls that benefit from this partnership with our dragons. Our dragons teach us how to value opposing energies within us as part of a creative, life-sustaining process, as opposed to creating further inner fragmentation.

Our dragons provide us with an important wisdom that teaches us the value of opposites. Rather than promoting an endless internal war between the different parts of our psyches, our dragons teach us the importance of learning balance between them. The opposites serve to complement and balance each other, and part of our job is to teach ourselves how to value and preserve this inner tension as a source of energy, creativity, and wisdom.

Journaling

One of the values we are learning how to practice in inner work, is the value of generosity, and this is where we need to be able to rely on more than just our ego-ideals to quantify and make sense of all of this information. An important and primary value of inner work is to learn to respond to, rather than automatically reject, images that do not make sense to us in our waking life, or simply repulse us in some way. Our unconscious uses the language of symbols and images, primarily, rather than giving us a logical narrative that we can follow in a straight line. The reason for this is that if our ego tried to make sense of these images right away, it would most likely interpret them incorrectly or reject them altogether, because they do not fit with the story of ourselves that our ego is protecting. Our unconscious images have to work around this barrier, which is why we end up encountering many of their images and symbols in our dreams. This is why myths, fairy tales, symbols, dreams, synchronicity, art, music, dance, and poetry are so important. They speak more directly to our souls with less of an ego-filter to dilute their energy and the impact that they have on us. These things speak more directly to our own immediate experiences of intuition and the wisdom it provides us.

One of the reasons why it is beneficial for us to learn how to read stories mythologically, meaning that we interpret the different characters of a story as all belonging to one psyche (our own), is that this gives us some experience and practice with our own soul work. In fact, anytime we read a myth and interact with it meaningfully, we *are* doing soul work. When we read these great stories, they invite us to explore the grandeur of the Heavens and scour the depths of Underworld. The images, the characters, and the creatures in these myths and fairy tales all mirror back to us some components of our own psyches, teaching us something about ourselves. If we can learn to recognize these different parts of us, in the projections of these myths, we can begin to make them more conscious within ourselves.

One method of capturing these images and working with them meaningfully is through a journaling process where we learn how to give voice to all of the different parts of our psyches. Journaling can help us not only identify their different parts, but also different stories about ourselves they have been carrying for us. When we journal about our dragons and allies, we are bearing witness to them. Rather than fighting or ignoring them, we acknowledge and interact with them. Journaling is one way we can put the virtue of curiosity into action. It can also teach us how to tame our dragons.

Inner work is a process where we learn to identify and agree to cultivate a healthy relationship with all of the different parts of our psyches, whether we regard them initially as dragons, allies or something more neutral. When engaged in journaling work, we can begin to observe how our inner characters play out familiar story lines. The journal gives us a chance to teach these different parts a new way to interact with these stories or learn to let them go when we begin to recognize that they are no longer serving our lives well. It also allows us to exercise some creativity in giving life to the new stories that desire to be born within us.

The journal process can also provide us with a space for dialogue between different parts of ourselves. Dialogue is necessary when a dragon appears, as we need to teach the other parts of our psyche to accept and befriend it. Dialogue allows us to see our situation from the different point of views of the inner characters of the psyche. It reminds us that there is more to us, more to life and more to whatever situation we find ourselves in, than our immediate reaction to them. Dialogue gives us a tool to be able to see initial feelings of the impossibility of our predicaments in life and tell a different story.

To use an example, let us suppose that we identify within ourselves a dragon that carries a story about perfectionism, and that this story feels particularly punishing, critical and overly judgmental. Our first instinct is to say, "I wish I could get rid of my perfectionism!" The problem is that we risk rejecting all the ways that this part of us contributes to our overall well-being in positive and life-giving ways. The story that we must let go is that this part of ourselves is supposed to be activated all the time and that we are always supposed to feel ashamed of it. In doing journaling work, we can learn to not only value this part of us but allow ourselves to choose when to use it when it is most helpful, as well as learn how to quiet it when it is not.

When we do this, we repurpose the dragon's energy from protecting the shaming story, and instead teach it to protect the part of the psyche that is responsible for valuing high quality and high performance. We learn also how to bring balancing relationships to different parts of ourselves. In this instance, it is beneficial for the part of our psyche that values high quality to have a good working relationship with another part that values and is responsible for spontaneity and play. Rather than being antagonists, trying to assert themselves over one another, they learn to value each other's input, temper one another, and recognize situations when one is called to take the lead, while the other gives the right of way, and vice versa. Each of our parts have their strengths and their limitations. Our task is to love and value all of them appropriately for what they are and have to offer, not punish them for what they are not.

The journal is where we begin to really explore all the different parts of ourselves that guide our lives, how we feel about ourselves and others, and how we experience the world. The journaling process is designed to help give voice to these inner characters and invite them into our awareness and active participation in our lives. It gives us a process to not only learn about our own dragons, but to bring them into helpful and life-giving interactions with the rest of our soul's eco-system.

Stream of Consciousness

Often the best way to begin is to just start writing. It may involve writing many words, pages or thoughts that just need to get out onto the paper. It may also involve nothing more than jotting down a single word or phrase that is important to you to remember and sit with for a while, perhaps returning to explore in more depth and detail later. It may not even be a word, but a symbol or a doodle or a picture of something that feels important to you. It is important not to censor yourself too much when you begin. Honor the value of what your soul needs to express without first needing to understand what it means or what it is worth. You are learning how to trust the process of your own soul. It will reveal to you exactly what you need to see, as long as you are willing to pay attention and spend some time with it.

In some cases, when you begin to identify different aspects of your psyche it will be apparent to you immediately whether or not the part that is trying to get your attention is a dragon. Other times, it may not be so obvious. It does not matter either way. You do not have to have it figured out before you begin writing and giving it a voice. The most important thing is that you give it a voice, let it tell you how it is feeling, and begin to understand its relationship to the stories about yourself that you carry. Here again, your soul is teaching you to trust your intuition before your reason, giving you permission to just follow your nose.

The journal is also a good place for you to record any dream imagery that feels particularly powerful to you. Again, it is more important to simply write down the dream before trying to make any sense of it. Remember that your soul wants you to learn how to sit with its images for a while before you make an attempt to decipher what they all mean. The reason for this is that it becomes easier for us to reject these images and hence reject our dragons when our ego-ideals go to work on them. Dreams can be a very rich source of wisdom for us, if we learn how to listen to them. Many people complain that they never remember their dreams, but there is actually a way for us to learn how to remember them more often.

When I was in graduate school, I was taking a class in Jungian studies, and one of our assignments for the class was to keep a dream journal. Immediately, half of the hands went up in the classroom (mine among them). We had a simple question: "What if I don't remember my dreams?" We were all worried about our ability to complete the assignment, and certainly worried about how this would affect our grades. I remember my professor flashed one of those smiles that communicates that he knows something that we don't know. His advice to us was to write something down in the journal anyway. He told us that he bet we would begin remembering our dreams within a couple of days.

Being the Western, rationalist male that I have been raised and trained to be, I was almost eager to debunk his theory of sudden recall and prove my professor wrong. It did not work. I began remembering my dreams, in great detail, within three days of writing something down each day in the morning after I woke up. Morning is the best time to record dream images, as they are fresh in your mind, and your waking mind has not fully kick-started the day's agenda in your head. Once we begin to pay attention to our unconscious, it knows it. Once we begin to pay attention to what is there, even if it is just under the surface, we begin to see it. Our unconscious feels less inhibited about sending more images our way. We can begin, if we wish, to build a very fruitful and vibrant dream life.

Dragons and Allies: An Inner Dialogue

Once we begin to get a better idea of what we're working with when we begin to journal, we can learn to identify more clearly the different parts of our soul trying to express themselves. Whether we identify a dragon or any ally (or something more neutral), it is helpful to give that part of us a name and a brief description; to give it a little biography. Naming the different parts of ourselves makes them more real to us. It helps to concretize these parts in our awareness, rather than allowing them to linger in spaces of ambiguity. This makes it easier and more productive to begin doing our work with them.

The first part of journaling needs no mental or emotional preparation from us, as we just want to express freely, and without conditions, exactly how we are feeling and what is showing up in our awareness that we need to pay attention to. The second part of journaling, which would be the *inner dialogue*, requires us to be a little more mindful in our approach. Our attitude, when doing a dialogue, should be one of curiosity rather than judgment. When we begin to judge the parts of ourselves that need to express themselves in a dialogue, we are more likely to inhibit them from expressing themselves fully. Remember, that our task when dealing with a dragon is not to respond to it with fight or flight, but to rather listen to what it has to say, even when it is not easy. Using curiosity and mindfulness, it relieves the mandates of our ego-ideal from having to weigh in with undue judgment or shame. We can remain curious and emotionally detached from them at the same time. This may take a little practice to get used to the idea, but practice is also what the journal itself is designed to promote.

The dialogue is intended for two or more of our parts of the psyche to talk to each other. Generally speaking, it works best if you limit a dialogue between two parts at a time. Through the dialogue, they have an opportunity to express how they are feeling and interact with each other. There is no right or wrong way to do a dialogue, but I have found it to be helpful to draw a line down the middle of the page, letting one part speak for itself on one side and another part speak on the other. To see them together on the same page helps us to solidify that this is a relationship that we are cultivating, reflecting the truth that our diverse parts do not operate in isolation from one another, and that cultivating a healthy inner community is our goal.

It is important that the interaction between two parts of your psyche also remain curious and free of judgment. The goal in a dialogue is not for one part to exert its superiority over another part, to get into conflict with or try to correct or fix the other. The job of each part is to express itself authentically, share empathy and compassion when necessary and just simply to bear witness to one another. We often underestimate just how powerful it is when we bear witness to each other. To bear witness is to fully see and hear someone exactly as they are. While we are free to do a dialogue between two parts of our soul that we already recognize as allies, or at the very least, appear neutral to us, it can be dangerous to attempt a dialogue between two of our dragons. After all, these parts are appearing to us as antagonists, which means we have some work to do with them. The work we must do in a dialogue with our dragons is to pair them with a part of our soul that we already recognize as an ally. Our allies need to be the ambassadors from our souls that greet our dragons for the first time and welcome them.

It is in our best interest to form a healthy, ongoing relationship between one of our dragons and one of our allies. Even after we have transformed a dragon into an ally, we need to remember that one of the energies the dragon asks us to integrate within our psyche is the energy of opposites. Our dragons provide us with the necessary opposites within our psyches that we must continue to balance time and time again. This ongoing partnership between an ally and a befriended dragon gives each of them an opportunity to practice balance. While it is important that they not try to dominate or correct each other, they do have a function of being able to observe each other's blind spots and inform each other of how each of them sees the world differently in any given situation. They also learn to mutually yield to each other as they learn when and where their voices need to be prominent and when they need to withdraw.

I will provide an example of this kind of dialogue from my own life. An ally that I recognized within myself years ago, takes on the form of a *Jedi Knight* from the great Star Wars mythology. For me, the Jedi symbolizes strength and wisdom. The Jedi carries the ability to be thoughtful and wise as well as the ability to become a formidable warrior when need be. The lightsaber, that a Jedi uses for defense and combat, became a symbol of *decisiveness* for me. This character represents the part of me that can cut to the heart of the matter, cut through the bullshit, and cut to the chase. This is a part of me that feels very strong, confident and able to use wisdom *and* discernment, even under trying circumstances.

Meanwhile, my Shadow was carrying a character of its own that was exerting a lot of power in my life, but not in a helpful way. I identified this dragon as a *Helpless Waif*. This is a part of myself that felt very afraid, needy and ill-equipped to handle the world. This is the part of myself that carried all my shame and insecurity. I identified this part of myself as having a wounded feminine quality. Having been taught my whole life, as a boy and a man, to deny such parts of myself, it is no surprise that I had hidden her very deep down in the shadows. Because I experienced this part of myself as a serious threat to my ego-ideal; and therefore, my self-confidence, happiness, and well-being, I identified this helpless waif as a dragon causing me pain. I was deeply ashamed of her. This was a part of me that always crumbled under pressure and felt very helpless and powerless. When I was first made aware of her, my reaction, quite frankly, was one of contempt and disgust.

Feelings of shame, disgust, terror, contempt, and even indifference are common feelings we can expect to experience when greeting our dragons for the first time. It is important that we are prepared for that. I had a lot of work to do with this particular dragon, and it took a period of time to allow myself to learn more about her and what particular gift she was trying to bring to me that I would eventually come to understand was a vital component of my birthright. In time, I learned first of all, that this part of me just wanted to be loved and taken care of, like all of the other parts of me. She was tender and fragile, yes, but I soon learned that this was part of her strength. I learned that when I took good care of her and kept her safe, she was capable of the most tremendous acts of compassion, empathy, and vulnerability. This is a part of myself that has allowed me to be intuitive and attentive to the woundedness in others.

My Jedi and my Helpless Waif could not be more diametrically opposed to each other, and yet, these are the two characters I rely on most to work together as a therapist. I need the strength of the decisive Jedi to team up with the deep empathy and vulnerability of the Waif, who is no longer feeling "helpless." Together they produce a wisdom and compassion far greater than could be produced apart. I am convinced, to this day, that if I had not done the work I needed to do with my Waif, then I would not be a very good therapist. These are two characters that I often bring together in my own dialogue. I still must work hard, sometimes, to take the best care of my Waif that I can. It is not always easy, and sometimes I can still become impatient with her. Our dragons call us into a continual and intentional engagement with them, but this is for our benefit. It ensures that we value these inner relationships and keep them alive, rather than taking them for granted. Just like outward relationships, if they are ignored, they tend to fall apart quickly and revert back to old habits.

Because dragons are so powerful, and because many of us have accumulated so many in our lives, it is often far easier for us to identify dragons than allies. They grab our attention much more quickly. It is important, however, that we take the time to learn about our allies, even if we are convinced that we do not have any. This is where the tool of projection can become useful for us in terms of looking for where our alchemical gold is showing up. If we can identify our gold in the face of another, whether it is a real person or a character of fiction, we can begin to capture some hints about the nature of our own gold and hence our own inner allies. That can be enough for us to begin to write about them. If we commit ourselves to the ethic of curiosity about our own projected gold, eventually our soul will reveal more of its nature to us, which will help us come to accept and embrace it as *our* gold over time.

The "Self"-Reflection

Once a dialogue has taken place, it is good to then invite the Self (i.e. Psyche, Soul, the sum of all of your parts), to reflect on the dialogue between your ally and your dragon. The Self is there to acknowledge and validate *all* its diverse parts and to convey to them that they are welcome and valued. The Self then begins to empathize with what your dragon and your ally each have to say about what is going on in your life at that moment in time, and you write this "Self"-reflection down in your journal. In addition to acknowledging the value of each individual part, the Self then acknowledges the value of the *relationship* between them, especially between your dragon and your ally. It blesses their ongoing alliance and the job they have to help us learn to balance important paradoxical tensions in our lives. You write down this blessing from the Self in your journal as well.

A dialogue accompanied by a "Self"-reflection can be a wonderful way to bring some balance and perspective into your life without having to judge or suppress any part that needs to be expressed. It can also help foster inner healing as it provides an opportunity for reconciliation from our inner fragmentation. It is a very generous and life-giving exercise for you to do. It is also a great way for you to become more familiar with all the different parts of yourself, be they dragons, allies, or more neutral characters. You begin to get very familiar with which parts of you are likely to be triggered in different situations in life. You also learn, through this familiarity and acceptance, to be less afraid of the dragon-like parts of you over time, as you are learning how to tame them appropriately, using their energy in creative and life-giving ways.

This journaling process is ultimately intended to invite more peace, balance, compassion, authenticity, wisdom, and strength into our lives. It does not necessarily solve all our problems, nor is it always intended to do so, but it does help us to heal festering wounds and invite inner peace. It does not save us from uncomfortable truths, painful feelings and experiences, but rather sheds a light on them, revealing to us the stories of ourselves that we carry and making us fully aware of the power and value of all of the parts of the psyche as they help us to actualize the life-giving stories we are trying to give birth to, as well as foster the death of the destructive stories that are harming us and holding us back from our own soul work and growth.

The Ground of All Being

As I have mentioned earlier in the book, soul work is our active acknowledgment and participation in the deeper, often unseen regions of our souls, making all the aspects of our souls conscious to us. We will never run out of life to live while we are discovering everything there is to know about our own souls. Soul work is the transformation process we must go through to remember what we have initially forgotten about ourselves. It is the work of recapturing the wholeness that belongs to us and is our birthright. Soul work is about practicing a vibrant, creative, and purposeful life. Soul work reminds us that there will always be more for us to discover about ourselves. Soul work engages our natural curiosities to invite us on a journey of discovery.

Our dragons appear to us in order to upset the homeostatic balance of our lives, when the stories of ourselves are no longer serving us well. Upsetting the internal balance serves the function of making us feel uncomfortable, and when we get uncomfortable, we tend to get moving. Taming a dragon requires a strength and resilience that must be practiced over time with patience and fortitude. If we offend our dragons during the process, we must be willing to come back and make the necessary amends to restore our relationship with them to continue our journeys. We need their energy and vitality, and we need their wisdom.

Just as we learn to listen to the proverbial angels in the lofty heights, we learn to hear from our dragons in the shadowy depths. Our job is always to come back to *earth*, however, and bring the lessons from each of the etheric realms with us when we return to the ground. The earth of our lives are the many daily rituals we choose to perform to stay alive and healthy; to work and to play; to love and to serve others. These rituals may seem uninteresting or banal to us, but if we suddenly stopped performing them, we would deteriorate or die. We need to eat food, sleep, exercise, work, pay bills, make love, teach our children, learn new skills, brush our teeth, etc. Our soul work does not supplant these activities to bring us a more fulfilling life. It keeps us more fully grounded in them. Our soul work is designed to help us do all of these things with more consciousness and purpose. After our time in the lofty Heavens and scouring the dark Underworld, we must come back to earth and live out the wisdom we have received there in our everyday lives. This reflects the truth of an old Zen proverb which states, "Before enlightenment, chop wood and carry water. After enlightenment, chop wood and carry water."

Taming dragons and learning how to tend to them with ongoing care takes continued practice and patience on our part. We often forget, and need to be reminded again and again, that it is the places in our lives that we neglect for too long that eventually become those dragons designed to get our attention, so that we "snap out of it" and get moving. The good news is that when we learn to do our dragon work, we get better at listening and attending to them over time. We learn better how to recognize the gifts they have for us and to receive them with increased openness and gratitude. We learn, also, the good rhythms we must balance between heaven, earth and the underworld. We become adept at paying close enough attention to our souls to know when it is time to move into and out of each of those places.

The function of myth and the mythological imagination, again, is to reveal to us the deepest truths of our own humanity. These stories govern not only how we perceive and feel about ourselves; they also govern how we choose to act and respond to each other in the world. Stories are important. Stories are powerful. Life-giving stories can help us grow and nurture ourselves better. Life-denigrating stories can destroy us. Whether the stories we are living are life-giving or destructive, the *telling* of our stories is important. It is important that we reinforce life-giving stories. It is also important that we bear witness to the destructive stories of ourselves, so that we can allow them die and make room for more authentic, life-giving stories that are a more accurate reflection of the fullness of our souls, allowing us to reclaim our inner gold, and live out our bliss more fully in the world.

Chapter 20
Taming Dragons: The Outer Work

One of the criticisms often leveled against inner work is that it is too self-centered and self-interested. The critique is not without its merit. Inner work represents one end of those important paradoxical tensions we must learn to balance in our lives. If we spend too much time there, and not enough time attending to our daily tasks in the outer world, the work becomes stale and ineffective. When this occurs, we can indeed be accused of "navel-gazing."

If the work we do in our inner lives had no consequences in the outside world, it might remain an interesting exercise, but not much more. At worst, it creates a callousness for the world around us and the people in it. We lose sight of the purpose of our compassion, which is not just to serve ourselves, but to serve our world as well. I often challenge the notion that inner work is not necessary for learning ethical ways of living in the world by suggesting that the best gift we could ever give to the world around us is the best and fullest version of ourselves possible. When we are connected to our bliss, we are connected to the energy necessary for us to be a vibrant source of compassion, mercy, justice, and generosity in the world. When we fail to take good care of ourselves and our souls, we lose sight of this healing energy. We become inert and ineffective, not only to the world but to ourselves as well. To suggest that self-care and an ability to care for others are two mutually exclusive concepts is to promote a false dichotomy. If we are not doing both, we will burn ourselves out.

When we do our inner work, we are also modeling for ourselves and others, how to work together in the outer world. If it is true that all wars begin in the human heart, then it follows that preventing our wars must include an ability to bring peace to our own inner wars. We learn how to connect with others by learning first how to connect with ourselves. We learn how to practice empathy and compassion with others by first learning how to exercise those virtues within ourselves. We learn how to love others also by first learning how to love ourselves.

The inner work we do can help us locate resistances and wounds that stand between us and discovering what we are meant to do in the world. It can activate the various vocations we are being called to in the world. When we are able to tend to our own wounds and bring healing to our own inner fragmentation, we clear away the debris that prevents us from connecting with our life's purpose.

Inner work is not a selfish pursuit. Rather, it provokes us to practice humility and the courage to recognize our life's purpose and then to act on it. I propose, however, that it is not fear of our own selfishness that prevents us from doing work, but our fear of *self-knowledge*. I believe also, that most of us are much more frightened of what we are actually capable of, then of what we are not. Inner work teaches us to look into these wounded places and shed light on them. Most of us, however, have learned to avoid seeing these places and discovering the deeper truths about ourselves, and we have developed many creative ways to avoid the calling of our own souls. One of the most effective avoidance mechanisms we have learned to employ is "busyness."

I believe that busyness has become the pathology of the modern world. We seem to have confused hard work with being busy and they are not necessarily the same thing. Hard work requires active and conscious engagement in a task with a purpose. Busyness is an avoidance mechanism, and for a Western world that so thoroughly and brutally rejects its own shadow, it should not be too surprising to us that it produces busyness as a virtue to which we believe we must all aspire. Our devotion to busyness reflects our fears of scarcity and fuels our need to consume and acquire things we believe will provide comfort and security (which ends up creating more discomfort and anxiety in the end). It is one of the reasons we experience our shadows as an evil threat that we must conquer or suppress. We can avoid discomforts of this magnitude for a period of time, but sooner or later our dragons catch up with us, and we are forced to deal with them and the discomfort they bring to initiate our journeys of the soul.

Paying deeper attention to the work of the soul does not require more time or energy, it requires us to recognize and listen to what is already there trying to speak to us. The energy we are expending is all being invested in the avoidance of our discomfort and the suppression of our shadows. If we no longer needed to expend our energy on avoidance, we would find that we have more than enough time and energy to engage in soul work.

The richness and depths of our souls are working hard to convey to us that they are wells of deep abundance, not scarcity, and when we learn how to operate out of that ground of being we will practice that ethic in the outside world. Our souls call us to learn how to trust them, not for the sake of eternal security and a life free from risk or pain, but to trust that we already have what we need inside of us to live abundant lives of purpose and growth, and that we are capable of healing wounds and inner reconciliation after life does knock us down. We may never be the same after such events, but this does not mean that our lives are over. For many of us it may be that are lives are really and fully about to begin. Wounds initiate journeys of the soul, not in the ways that we planned or expected, but sometimes in the ways that we most need.

Doing our own inner work is also a recognition that we are important and that we matter. Most of us are scarcely aware of the impact that we have on others from day-to-day. Most of us will never know all the ways in which we have meaningfully touched the lives of others. It can become very easy to take ourselves for granted. We have all come to believe that 'celebrity' is the only way to make a meaningful impact on the world, but this is an illusion. Whether we like or not, we are impacting and influencing others every day in the world of ordinary lives with ordinary tasks that are nevertheless, very important. When we take that truth seriously, we are more likely to take seriously the necessity of our own soul work.

Whether we accept this truth or not, we are all contributing to the state of the world that we live in, both for good or for ill. If we are living in constant fear and shame of our shadows and our dragons, we will not be able to do our own inner reconciliation work, and we will project the wrath of our dragons onto the world around us. Our inner work matters to the world. We will not be able to be lovers and healers of a wounded world without first learning to become lovers and healers of ourselves.

We can see so much evidence of our own inner fragmentation and undealt-with dragons projected out into the world. We see it in our politics and economic principles. We see it in so many of our religious institutions. We see it played out daily on the news. We see it paraded around as bargaining chips in institutions of power. We see it in everyone else except ourselves, and this is where we fail our species, because we are all so busy blaming each other that we are unable to examine all the ways we are contributing to and sustaining our half-world. If we have not yet learned to assess our own worth as individual humans, we will be incapable of assessing the worth of others, and we will be blind to the work our own souls have for us to do in the wider world around us.

It is not because we exist in an endless state of brokenness and sin, rendering us helpless, that we continue to perpetuate old stories and myths about us that need to die. It is because we fail to see ourselves accurately and recognize the inherent wholeness that is our birthright. It is because we refuse our journeys of the soul to return to our own inner worth, gold and bliss with consciousness and purpose that we find ourselves stuck in seemingly endless loops of brokenness and despair. This does not have to be the case, however. We all have the power within us to do this work. We have all been instilled with this birthright because of our humanity, not in spite of it. It is time for us to learn how to take responsibility for ourselves. It is time to take responsibility for our dragons and let them do their part to help us repair our inner fragmentation.

Our lives, again, are a gift to the world around us. The things that excite and motivate us the most are likely the gifts of the soul trying to reveal their purpose to us. The best gift we can give to the world is to, in the words of Joseph Campbell, "Follow our bliss." Our bliss informs our purpose in life. When we deny our bliss, we deny our gifts to the world, and we are more likely to live anxious and unfulfilled lives. When we wake up to who and what we really are, as we are, we begin to participate in our own joy, and we are compelled to express that joy in the world.

The world needs us to do our work and tame our dragons. The world needs us to bring healing and reconciliation to our inner fragmentation. The world is desperately calling on us to learn how to love ourselves again with humility and purpose. The world desires us to see the beauty in ourselves so that we can finally see its beauty. The world is calling on us to reconnect with the Divine Feminine we have so thoroughly rejected and wake up from the Half-lives we have constructed with all of its institutions, empires and greedy men seeking to reap from it all that they can, while turning a blind eye to their own sisters and brothers and the earth that sustains all of us.

We are not called to be endlessly broken and fragmented. The only sin we keep committing is the sin of not seeing ourselves accurately, as whole people with birthrights to claim, and there is nothing original about that particular sin. When we stop acting out of our own inner fragmentation and reclaim our birthrights, then we start treating others differently. Remember that we will rise to our own expectations of ourselves. If that expectation is that we are forever evil and broken, then this is how we can expect ourselves to behave in the world. If our expectation, rather, is that we are creatures of wholeness designed for deep love and purpose, then we will rise to that expectation and act accordingly.

When we learn to recognize and reclaim our own inner gold, we begin to act out of a deep love for humanity and the world itself. We stop acting out of fear; whether that be a fear of scarcity, a fear of hell, or the fear of the wrath of our own shame. When we do our soul work, we learn how to really recognize and honor the divine in all living people and creatures, and this is the healing medicine our world needs. It is the healing of our own souls. If we can summon the courage to work with our own shadows and tame the dragons they produce, then we begin to learn the healing art of inner reconciliation and peace, because we have been able to secure powerful allies for ourselves with a vibrant energy that can be utilized for the healing of our souls and our world, rather than its further fragmentation and destruction.

We have a long and rich history as Western people with the corresponding myths that have both risen and fallen throughout time. There are many gifts in those traditions for us to reclaim as well as many untended wounds and points of arrested development that we have yet to heal. Our soul work is not simply for our own benefit. Never before have we been aware of just how interconnected we are as a species. Never before have we been aware of just how fragile and delicate our earth is, and the impact that we have (and continue to have) on it. The process that we undertake on an individual level with our soul work is also a process that must continue to take place on a collective scale as well. We cannot expect our culture to grow, change, evolve and make the necessary shifts of consciousness to better protect ourselves and our planet without first learning this process on an inner, individual level. What we do and who we are matters.

If we cannot recover the divine purpose of our souls and learn to do our dragon work, then this will have consequences for us and our entire world. Dragon-taming is serious business. Fortunately, if we learn the language of our own souls, including that of our dragons, taking on the tasks of the work has been put before us yields an incredibly rewarding and sustaining fruit. Do we have the courage to do what it takes to rediscover our own gold? Can we be brave enough to learn how to tame dragons and become deep reservoirs of consciousness, curiosity, love and compassion? Are we willing to risk perhaps letting go of old stories about ourselves that no longer make sense or serve us well? The pearl of great price is never far away. It is always there, and always has been there, waiting for us to accept it. We need only choose it.

It is time for us, as Western people, to learn how to tame and befriend our own dragons. Our myths are beginning to change, and they are forcing us to grow up. We have mastered the ethics and virtues of the half-world long enough. Our birthrights are calling us into a new paradigm and a new way of dealing with our dragons. To think about what we could accomplish together if we learn how to do this is exciting and refreshing. The choice belongs to us, however. Nobody else can do this work for us. Will we answer the call of our souls' deepest purpose for us to reclaim our birthrights, or will we continue to linger in our half-worlds? The world is producing the right dragons, at the right time, for us to become conscious of this choice. The next move is ours.

Conclusion

We have great work to do, both in our individual and collective Western psyches. It is good, life-giving work, however. It is healing work. It is the kind of work that calls us to pay attention to our own stories and myths, which continue to guide us and show us where we need to go and how we need to continue to grow as we learn to reclaim our birthrights.

Our myths are the stories that we are living and also the stories that are living us at the same time. Myth is the ultimate paradoxical tension that gives us life. We create it and are created by it. These are the stories of the soul in every aspect and manifestation of it from the light to the shadow and all of the spaces in between. Myths are alive and active, growing and evolving with us, mirroring back to us the truths about where we have been and where we are going. Myths show us the "already, but not yet" qualities of the human journey out of our gardens of innocence and unconsciousness, through the wilderness, and ultimately returning back to ourselves with consciousness and purpose.

We know that the reality of our own human shadows is not a negotiable one. They exist whether we like it or not. We can ignore and fight our shadows if we choose, but this comes at a cost to us. The prices we pay are the dragons that are birthed when we ignore our own shadows for too long. We pay a further price if we continue to ignore or fight our own dragons as well.

In our Western myths, we have a strong heritage of shadow denial and conquest, often appearing in the form of dragons that must be slain in order to bring peace. Our Western myths reflect and often glorify the virtues of the Half-Man and his world, confusing this inner fragmentation with a state of wholeness. Because many of our Western myths are focused on this shadow-denial, we continue to perpetuate a virtue of brokenness in our modern world, failing to acknowledge our own projections and take responsibility for them. In the world of the Half-Man, we reject our own darkness, the Divine Feminine, and ultimately, we reject the nature of our own souls; ever striving instead to conquer our own human nature rather than embody it. We see the effects of this ethic of divide and conquer all around us. Our earth, our very home, is being daily poisoned by it.

I believe, however, that things are beginning to change, and in this lies our hope. Deep, unconscious forces within our souls are beginning to stir our natural curiosity again, a curiosity that has been deeply buried beneath a punishing ethic of personal piety, dogmatic institutionalism, and an unquestioned allegiance to the status quo. Our curiosity, if we allow it, breathes new life into us once more. I have argued in this book that curiosity is the antidote to pervasive fear and shame. Mindfulness allows us to temper our immediate judgments about ourselves and the world, which are governed in no small part by our ego-ideals. These are tools that allow us to practice healing, reconciliation and peace within ourselves and with each other.

The Fire That Never Dies is continually at work in our lives. It relates to us both the impermanence of all things, as well as the importance of all things in their appropriate place and time in our lives. Our dragons exist to push us into that fire when we become too reluctant, too distracted, or too complacent. We are not meant to find a permanent solution for all the troubles, missteps and discomforts that we experience in life. Neither are we meant to hang onto old hurts and wounds for too long and withhold true joy and ecstasy from ourselves as we learn to enjoy all the sweetness that life has to offer.

Being opened to learning more about ourselves from all the diverse and creative parts of our own psyches, even our dragons, offers us a richness and depth to human life that is best understood and articulated through art, symbols, myths and vibrant, life-giving rituals, as well as meaningful community. Learning the language of symbol and myth is part of how we grow in wisdom and wholeness throughout our lives. Learning the language of symbol and myth is what allows us to experience life in the most savory of ways, for we are both learning and experiencing the deepest truths of our nature and shared humanity through them.

Healing begins when we learn to listen to ourselves and honor all our different parts, both dragons and allies. Our dragons bring to us the necessary conundrums we need at the right time to deal with something that we have not yet dealt with. When we learn to listen to the wounded parts of ourselves with kindness and wisdom, they are then allowed to heal and transform. When those parts of us are allowed to heal, we allow old stories about ourselves that no longer serve us well to die. This clears the space in our hearts to create the new stories about ourselves that are trying to emerge. When we listen to what our dragons must say, they cease to be our adversaries and become our companions and protectors.

We are all living in a very tumultuous and uncertain time in the history of our species. I believe that the status quo, governed and nurtured by the structures of a punishing patriarchy for so long, is beginning to shift and crumble. An awareness of Sophia and her great importance to us is being re-awoken from the collective unconscious. Social, religious, sexual, and relational norms are all beginning to move and shift beneath our feet, and these shifts, I believe, are long overdue. While there is always hope for great promise and abundance that are possible when these large paradigm shifts occur, it also rattles the institutions built on the status quo so remarkably as to instigate panic and fear, and there are always those ready in waiting to capitalize off our fears to feed their own greed. Those invested in the unbalanced status quo of a split and broken Western psyche will fight to keep the privileges they have gained. Learning how to both listen and temper our inner warriors will be of paramount importance. We must learn to do our inner work to stay strong in the midst of a world in chaos, learning to adjust to these shifts, while ushering in new stories and myths about who we are as a species.

Unless we can begin to bring healing to the wars that exist inside our own individual hearts and minds, we cannot expect to bring our outer wars to an end. We are living in a world that is begging us to attend to our inner fragmentation and do the work to begin mending it. Courage, compassion, resilience, wisdom, and humility is called for, with every one of us. There are no guarantees that our efforts to bring peace and justice into the world will keep us safe. This is the risk we take in standing up for the beauty and inner royalty of ourselves and all life that sustains us. We must decide, together, if it is worth the risk. I believe that it is, and I believe our contribution toward the care and healing of our souls and the world itself requires our ability to know how to acknowledge and befriend our own dragons.

Book Endorsement by: Dr. Harley Ferris

"In an attempt to understand ourselves and our place within a Western society, our collective desire to reconcile the various, conflicting parts of our human nature clashes with our need to essentialize or categorize the human condition. As a result, our common wisdom has become increasingly more narrow and banal, reflecting the egocentric, masculine, and positivist ideals that structure our cultural and social perspectives.

The Fire That Never Dies is a greatly needed antidote to conventional wisdom and feel-good self-help advice, eloquently exhorting us not only to resist ignoring, fleeing, or fighting the shadows within us but to in fact explore, embrace, and harness those parts of ourselves that frighten us most, so that we may better understand and employ every facet of our being.

With echoes of Joseph Campbell, James Hillman, and Thomas Moore, author Matthew Markell deftly weaves storytelling, psychology, and philosophy into a compelling explication of myths and monsters that humans have created in our own image to name that which we fear, demonstrating that the menagerie of dragons we recognize only too well, are symbols of reconciliation rather than destruction.

This is a journey not of conquer but of compassion, of bringing our whole selves into one place instead of the fractured, compartmentalized individuals a Western culture all too easily produces. Through fascinating narratives, accessible theory, and practical application, Markell provides a clear map for those with the courage to follow through treacherous territory to a place of healing, reconciliation and peace."

~Dr. Harley Ferris
Assistant Professor of English, University of Findlay

End Notes

[i] Rainier M. Rilke, *Letters to A Young Poet (Revised Ed.)* (New York: W.W. Horton Company, Inc., 1954), 31.

[ii] Joseph Campbell: *The Hero with A Thousand Faces* (New York: Bollingen, 1949), 11.

[iii] William Shakespeare: *Hamlet, Act III, Scene I.*

[iv] Joseph Campbell: *The Hero with A Thousand Faces* (New York: Bollingen, 1949), 29.

[v] Doug Niles, *Dragons: The Myths, Legends and Lore* (Avon. Adams Media, 2013), 59-60.

[vi] Joseph Campbell: *The Hero with A Thousand Faces* (New York: Bollingen, 1949), 108.

[vii] Campbell: *The Hero*, 93.

[viii] Michael Meade: *Fate and Destiny: The Two Agreements of the Soul (2nd Ed.)* (Seattle: Greenfire Press, 2012), 135-136.

[ix] Garet Garrett: *Ouroboros* (New York: E.P. Dutton and Co., 1926), 1.

[x] Robert A. Johnson: *Balancing Heaven and Earth: A Memoir of Visions, Dreams and Realizations* (New York: HarperCollins, 1988)

[xi] Joseph Campbell: *The Hero with A Thousand Faces* (New York: Bollingen, 1949), 153.

[xii] Carl G. Jung: *The Archetypes and the Collective Unconscious* (Princeton: Princeton University Press, 1968), 20.

[xiii] Joseph Campbell: *The Hero with A Thousand Faces* (New York: Bollingen, 1949), 52.

[xiv] Sanford: *Evil*, 58-59.

[xv] Ibid, 64.

[xvi] Michael Meade: *Fate and Destiny: The Two Agreements of the Soul (2nd Ed.)* (Seattle: Greenfire Press, 2012), 136.

[xvii] Sanford: *Evil*, 105.

[xviii] Doug Niles: *Dragons: The Myths, Legends and Lore* (Avon: Adams Media, 2013), 13.

[xix] Joseph Campbell: *Pathways to Bliss: Mythology and Personal Transformation* (Novato: New World Library, 1996), 40.

[xx] Doug Niles: (2013). *Dragons: The Myths, Legends and Lore* (Avon: Adams Media, 2013), 143.

[xxi] Burton Raffel: (Tr.), *Beowulf* (New York: Signet Classics, 1963)

[xxii] Robert L. Stevenson: *The Strange Case of Dr. Jekyll and Mr. Hyde* (New York: Barnes and Noble Classics, 2003), 62.

[xxiii] Ibid, 63.

[xxiv] J.R.R. Tolkien: *The Hobbit (Revised Ed.)* (New York: Ballantine Books, 1982), 215-216.

[xxv] Thomas Moore: *Dark Nights of the Soul: A Guide to Finding Your Way Through Life's Ordeals* (New York: Gotham Books, 2004), 225.

[xxvi] Ibid, 155-156.

[xxvii] Robert Powell: *The Sophia Teachings: The Emergence of the Divine Feminine in Our Time* (New York: Lantern Books, 2001), 34.

[xxviii] Diana Ferguson: *Greek Myths and Legends* (London: Collins and Brown Ltd., 2000)

[xxix] Rollo May: *The Cry for Myth* (New York: Dell Publishing, 1991), p. 95

[xxx] Michael Meade: *The Water of Life: Initiation and the Tempering of the Soul (Revised Ed.)* (Seattle: Greenfire Press, 2006), 204.

[xxxi] Robert A. Johnson: *Balancing Heaven and Earth: A Memoir of Visions, Dreams and Realizations* (New York: HarperCollins, 1988), 62.

[xxxii] Joseph Campbell: *Pathways to Bliss: Mythology and Personal Transformation* (Novato. New World Library, 1996), 119.

[xxxiii] Thomas Moore: *Care of the Soul: A Guide for Cultivating Depth and Sacredness in Everyday Life* (New York: HarperCollins, 1986), 5.

[xxxiv] Noela Evans: *Meditations for the Passages and Celebrations of Life: A Book of Vigils* (New York: Belltower, 1994), 138.